W9-BYP-536

CAUGHT IN THE MIDDLE

Henry Libersat

CAUGHT IN THE MIDDLE

Meeting God in the
Midst of Problems

CROSSROAD · NEW YORK

1987

The Crossroad Publishing Company
370 Lexington Avenue, New York, N.Y. 10017

Printed in the United States of America

Library of Congress Cataloging in Publication Data

Libersat, Henry.
  Caught in the middle.

  1. Christian life—Catholic authors.   I. Title.
BX2350.2.L457   1987   248.4'82   87-5297
ISBN 0-8245-0822-X (pbk.)

To my own Peg,
my late mother, Elda,
and
Louise Primeaux, the teacher
who saw and nourished the potential.

Contents

	Special Thanks	ix
	Introduction	1
Chapter 1.	THE WITNESS OF SISTER BRIEGE	7
Chapter 2.	THE MINISTRY OF MOTHER ANGELICA	23
Chapter 3.	THE POWER OF FORGIVENESS	33
Chapter 4.	MAKING MARRIAGE CLICK	49
Chapter 5.	FINDING GOD IN THE MIDDLE	75
Chapter 6.	LET'S RETURN TO ORDINARY CHRISTIANITY	101
Chapter 7.	POWER TO HIS PEOPLE	117
Chapter 8.	A WORD ABOUT BISHOPS, PRIESTS AND DEACONS	129
Chapter 9.	FROM THE ROOFTOPS	151

Special Thanks

. . . to Peg, my wife, who pushed when I needed pushing, and inspired this book through her faith, love and fidelity over the last thirty-five years.

. . . to Michael Leach of Crossroad/Ungar/Continuum who provided editorial support and encouragement.

. . . to Dick Biow, one of those friends who challenges and encourages in the same breath.

. . . to Sister Briege McKenna and Mother Angelica whose ministry has given me new life and a greater insight into the mysteries of the Christian faith.

. . . to the community of St. Mary Magdalen Parish for giving me a place and a time to celebrate and increase my faith, love and hope, and especially to Father Paul Henry, pastor, whose leadership calls others to imitate his spirit of generous service.

. . . to Linda P. Rooney, Father David Ferguson, the people of the pastoral ministry program in the Orlando diocese, the staff of *The Florida Catholic*, and, last but not least,

. . . to my own little Spirit of God Community for love, support, joy, prayer and a place to be me however me happens to be at any given moment.

Introduction

Have you ever said to yourself, "I'm caught in the middle," and wished desperately that you were not? It is, of course, a familiar phrase. Everyone feels "caught in the middle."

Each of us, at one time or another, feels pressure from all sides. We yearn to be rescued from that uncomfortable, frustrating and sometimes frightening place we call "The Middle."

The Middle is where, as one evangelistic preacher put it, "the rubber meets the road." It's being "between a rock and a hard place."

Wives often find themselves caught between husband and children, between housewifery and careers, between a crying need for quiet time and the crying of babies or the whining of teen-agers and all the other demands of rearing a family.

Husbands feel "caught in the middle" between the agony of unfulfillment and the badly concealed temptation to junk it and flee to Hawaii.

Parents are caught in the middle between their desire to rear children properly and pressures from their peers and their children's peers. Parents of sick children and people in debt are desperately caught between a natural tendency to despair and a spiritual call to hope in an unseen and unknown God.

Young adults are caught in the middle between dreams of successful careers and unemployment; between professorial promises of great opportunities and mundane jobs for which they are academically overqualified; between a desire and need for a loving

1

relationship with a member of the opposite sex and the inability to make lasting commitments; between adolescence and maturity.

Many lonely older people struggle between hope in loved ones and life as shut-ins or shut-aways.

Alcoholics are caught in the middle between fear and a self-imposed and false sense of invincibility, between a desire to be whole and addiction to a drug that destroys wholeness.

Middle management is caught between employees and upper management; school teachers, between parental demands for better education and the rebellion of pampered, spoiled children.

Christians are caught in the middle between light and darkness, between the desire for unity and loyalty to denominations; perhaps the most telling and crucial Christian tension is to be caught between irresistible temptation and "sufficient grace."

U.S. Catholics, in particular, are torn between wanting to be recognized by bishops and pope as good Catholics and the pressures and the subtle nuances of a pluralistic society that challenge traditional faith and discipline. Christians interested in social justice (and what true Christian isn't?) are caught between liberation theology and sacramental spirituality, between the growing consciousness of the social Gospel and the rebirth of general desire for a personal, quiet, God-me spirituality.

There is a growing gulf between dedicated Christians who feel social justice is the ultimate in evangelization and those who believe justice will flow from a truly evangelical approach to preaching the scriptures.

Pastors find themselves in a Catch-22 situation as they struggle to do more pastoral work and less administration, finding that while lay people may have the secular skills to manage business, they lack a sense of Church, the ability to work in community, the pastoral sensitivity to run parish business without much pastoral supervision—and pastors find they are back in business, again!

Celibates are caught between a need for a personal, loving, holy, human lover and the desire to be a lover of many; married couples, between the demands of conjugality and the need for privacy.

And what of soldiers? What greater pressure than to desire peace with all one's heart, to fear death and to have to kill and chance being killed. Or the peace activist who must decide whether to break the law and go to jail as a sign of protest against the evils of war and the threat of nuclear annihilation.

I live in The Middle—as middle manager, as editor, as charismatic Catholic in a not-so-charismatic Church, as father of seven and grandfather of seventeen. Because of this experience in "The Middle," I've often quipped, "If ever I'm canonized I want to be the patron saint of people caught in the middle."

The Middle is a good place, not a bad one.

The Middle is the place where hearts make choices between love and hate, between justice and injustice, between faith and faithlessness, between good and evil of all sorts, between greatness and meanness, between hope and despair, between joy and mere pacification, between self and others.

The Middle is where life is lived in fullest power, in fullest consciousness of self and others. Or it is the place of disaster and defeat. The Middle is the place of decision, of self-determination, of the ultimate communion with other people and with God. Or it is the place of utter isolation and desolation.

People desperately want out of The Middle—but once out, they can't help but look back. Somehow they realize they have had a special brush with life. They are fascinated by what they saw and what they might have seen. So they look back with satisfaction or disappointment in themselves and in others. The Middle is a place for testing and tempering friendships, for challenging prejudices, for inviting people into a healing and forgiving experience.

The Middle is a very spiritual place. People caught in the middle have a spiritual experience as they struggle to make sense of opposing forces, of contradictions. In The Middle, people sharpen their spiritual insight. They need not be Christian to be spiritual. They need not be Buddhist. They can be agnostic or atheist. They are spiritual by nature.

But for Christians The Middle is the place where one learns what it means to die to self. It is the place where, finding no suitable answers in the human mind, the Christian looks to his Lord and seeks the perfect will.

This is the place for victory, this Middle that demands of Christians total surrender to the all-knowing and all-loving Crucified One. They see, in Jesus, one who lived and died in The Middle.

When Jesus faced Pilate, he was caught in the middle. He could have appeased Pilate; he could have appeased his people. But he chose integrity, to remain true to who he knew he was—the Son of God. He could not deny his Sonship without denying the Father. This Jesus could not do. Making his decision for the Father, in our name and in our place he hung in unspeakable agony on the Cross, the ignominious gibbet, the tree of shame, the throne of criminals and the despised.

And even on the Cross Jesus was still caught in the middle, between heaven and earth, between hope in his Father and despair, between loss of all faith and the greatest act of faith possible, between total rejection by his people and the chance for saving those who hated him.

On the Cross, he still had choices to make—to forgive or to condemn, to blaspheme or to bless.

We all know what he chose. He chose to forgive his people and his executioners. He chose to bless the Father. And as Satan prematurely danced the victory dance when Jesus breathed his last, the Father, Jesus and the Spirit opened the gates of paradise, called humankind into the fullness of God's glory.

I don't relish being caught in the middle. But I do appreciate The Middle. In The Middle, I have discovered my self-worth as I, with the Lord's great and generous help, defeated alcoholism, learned to love myself, discovered great hidden resources of strength and talents that could help change the world.

In was in The Middle that I learned I was not the great Super-Catholic Dad I thought I was, that it was not zeal for God but personal pride that had prompted me to drive a wedge between myself and my young adult children whose faith was not what I thought it should be. It was in The Middle that I found Sister Briege McKenna whose ministry let me feel, for the first time, the touch of the crucified hand deep in my spirit, whose ministry set me free to love, to be loved, to forgive and be forgiven, to heal and to be healed, to hear God's Word with new ears and an eager heart and to preach it with power, joy and authority.

It was in The Middle that I met Mother Angelica of Birmingham whose call to evangelization and whose generous Gospel spirit fanned into a flame the smothered desires of a young Louisiana farm boy to be a missionary for the Church and for God. In The Middle, I learned that community is a work, not a word; a purifying fire, not a warm fuzzy; a power that sends people into the unknown, not just a safe place.

If you are caught in the middle, praise God and seek him inside you, for he is there with you, in The Middle.

At our parish church, St. Mary Magdalen's, Altamonte Springs, Florida, there is a wooden walkway on the east side of the church that leads to a grotto of Our Lady. The planks of the walkway are nailed closely together, but not so closely that light cannot pass through from the sun to the soil below.

There is nothing very special about cracks between wooden planks. But still, in those little cracks, as unimportant and unnoticed as they are, small shoots of grass grow toward the sun. The cracks are "caught in the middle" between two planks, but they invite and nourish life. The small grasses growing in the cracks are caught between the same planks, but they produce oxygen and they gave a middle-aged man an insight into being caught in the middle.

If you are caught in the middle, praise God, for you are living fully and are on the verge of great personal revelation, personal self-discovery, another insight into family and friends, a deeper look into the heart of God.

If you are caught in the middle, please read on. In the next two chapters, I will share my own experiences in learning to deal with The Middle. I had two remarkable teachers—Sister Briege and Mother Angelica.

From their own example, spiritual direction and faith, I learned specifically to deal with suffering, to forgive myself for being a sinner. And much more.

So, for the rest of this book, I will try to share insights born of my relationship with my wife Peg, the two Sisters, and a score of other close and influential Christian friends. I will share stories of prisoners and single parents, of ministers and lay people.

In broken relationships, in the midst of money problems, in struggles against alcoholism and self-hatred, in the agony of facing single parenthood, in the struggles to learn to forgive, in the midst of rejection and failure—all are truly spiritual "places," places where God lives waiting to be found.

Frankly, some of what I share will be autobiographical testimony, for truth is concrete. But in that testimony I hope to convey the never-ending and hopefully contagious excitement I feel as I look for God, and find him, in The Middle.

I hope that this book helps you realize that you are not alone. I hope and pray that it helps you to learn or remember anew, in a more trusting fashion, that God comes to us where we are, especially in The Middle. For in truth, he is already there.

Chapter 1

THE WITNESS OF SISTER BRIEGE

What do you do when you are caught in the middle of a destructive habit?

What do you do when you're too afraid to admit your problem, afraid that if you admit your problem—whether it's adultery or alcoholism, crime or a crisis of faith—family and friends will not understand or, worse, desert you.

What do you do when you want help but are afraid that admitting your problem will make it harder for you to help your own family?

Where can you go for help?

Should I tell you what you already know, that there are civic and religious agencies that help people with such problems?

Should I tell you about Alcoholics Anonymous or Al-Anon or Narcotics Anonymous?

No, I am not going to talk about agencies and programs. These are good and necessary, but mine is a more fundamental and urgent message.

I want to tell you not to be afraid of yourself, your disease or of God. You don't have to be afraid of anything or anyone. Fear is what cripples you, leads you into patterns of behavior that cripple your spirit and even your body.

You can break out of addiction, sinful habits. I want you to know that God hears you when you ask, even cry, for help, that God heals, that prayer works, that you can be happy, sane and whole, that darkness flees before light.

I've felt the touch of God and I know these things are true.

October 31, 1976, is an important date for me. But it means nothing apart from who I was before and who I am after that experience with the "healing nun," Sister Briege McKenna, OSC, whose ministry changed my life and launched me into a career of Catholic evangilization, preaching and teaching.

Her ministry to me that Halloween morning is a milestone in my journey through life. In fact, I now divide my life into two periods— BB and AB—Before Briege and After Briege.

Briefly, the past as prologue . . .

I was born in Groves, Texas (near Port Arthur), and when I was eleven, my parents, native Louisianians, moved back to their home state.

In Louisiana, I was a very lonely young boy. At fifteen years of age, I was attracted to a beautiful thirteen-year-old Cajun girl, Peggy LeBlanc.

Peg had matured young, as many Cajun girls do.

It must be something in the spices or the bayou water or just in the blood.

Whatever, I knew the moment I saw her that I wanted to marry her.

Call it romantic nonsense and puppy love if you will, but we were married June 4, 1952—and that was thirty-five years ago. I was seventeen and Peg was fifteen. Our seven children are all grown and now there are seventeen grandchildren.

When we married I was in college. I quit after completing two years at Southwestern Louisiana Institute (now University of Southwestern Louisiana) in Lafayette.

Following college, we moved to Groves, Texas. There, I worked as a fence builder, roadway repairman, water-meter reader and garbage-truck driver. Our first two children were born there.

Being away from our parents gave us a sense of freedom. We soon began to change our life style. We dropped out of church, feeling that fishing and water-skiing were more fun than worship.

We were searching, trying to be grown up when we were still kids. Today most people don't even begin to think of marriage until they are twenty-three or twenty-four years of age. By that time, we were the parents of four children.

When our son David was a year old he became very sick. He dehydrated and his kidneys shut down.

He was dying. The doctor and the nurses were frantically trying to find a blood vessel large enough to take the medicine they hoped would activate his kidneys. Peg was crying and I was pacing the floor, angry and scared all at the same time.

Even though in the past I had been active in church, serving Mass, working in parish festivals and excelling in catechism, I didn't know how to pray—except for a few traditional prayers. I carried a rosary with me, and although I had not prayed in many, many months, that night I took the rosary out of my pocket and prayed!

I was afraid to go to God because I was a sinner. I wanted to make bargains and deals. So I went to the Mother of Jesus as I had been taught to do. I promised the Virgin Mary that if David lived not only would I come back to the Church but I would also work for the Church full time if God wanted me to.

Within a few minutes after making that vow, the doctor came out and said, "Your son will live."

I began attending daily Mass the very next morning; I read all the pamphlets in the magazine rack in the back of the church. I especially liked those written by the Fathers Miller of the Redemptorists in Ligouri, Missouri.

A year later we moved back to Louisiana, and I went to work for the Louisiana Department of Highways as an engineer's aide.

I began drinking heavily when I was working for the highway department. I commuted sixty miles round trip every day. It was then I began stopping off at one convenience store after another getting "one" and "one more" for the road. I even had charge accounts at a couple of the stores.

I was unhappy with the highway department. There was no creative challenge. I was working with people whose hands and minds built roads and highways. I loved to write, to draw, to dream. All through high school, although I was making A's in English, I wrote voluntary compositions "to bring up my grade." My love for writing, along with my new religious fervor, a natural fascination with theology and philosophy, and a deep thirst for peace, was to provide a way out of the unhappy work with the highway department.

When frustration with the Department of Highways reached a peak, I was in touch with the Father Alexander O. Sigur, editor of the *Southwest Louisiana Register*, the Catholic weekly for the Lafayette diocese. He had come to the Newman Center at the college in Lafayette just before I quit college. I told him I was interested in writing. He asked me to do three columns and outline nine others. I did. "A Letter from Pierre" was born. It was a general commentary column, about faith and hope and love—things I talked about a lot, things I wanted to understand, things present in kernel form, yet to grow through suffering, experience, peaks and valleys.

A year later, I went to work full time in the Catholic press, at twenty-five years of age. My entire family, except for Peg who didn't say no but could not say definitely yes, was against my going to work for the Church. My pastor was opposed as was my retreat director.

But I prayed, and for the first time in my life I thought I heard God say, "I'm calling you. You made a vow and I'm taking you up on it."

I worked ten years for the *Register*. Then we moved, for a very short time, to Huntington, Indiana, where I worked for *Our Sunday Visitor*. There, the drinking really became serious because we found ourselves, instead of in a new and challenging opportunity, stuck in the middle of a big company shakeup.

My good friend and agent, Bill Holub (now with XXIII Publications), told me about an opening at *The Florida Catholic* in Orlando.

I took the job and became managing editor of *The Florida Catholic*, which served two dioceses at that time. Now we serve five of Florida's seven dioceses.

The Libersat clan arrived in Orlando on October 11, 1969. The kids all graduated from high school and are scattered about the U.S. Only three remain in Florida.

All the while, until September 2, 1977, my drinking problem became more serious. Frequently I would black out and not be able to remember where I had been.

Amazingly, I never missed work because I was drinking. Most people didn't believe I was an alcoholic. Some people still refuse to believe I am an alcoholic.

But I am. When you drink enough to get drunk, I mean really staggering drunk, four or five times a week, when you can't stop until you've downed the last beer or drink, or until you pass out, you are an alcoholic.

I'm sober, now. And I thank God for that. My sobriety was slow in coming because I would not admit I was an alcoholic.

Sobriety was slow in coming, too, because part of my illness was a fear of reality, of wanting to push problems aside. I felt trapped, caught in the middle. I wanted to be a good husband and father, a good worker, a sober person, but pressures were too much for me. I did not believe I could cope. I was afraid to fail and therefore afraid to try.

I am convinced that it was Peg's steadfast love that finally helped me to sober up. It was her continuous love that finally proved to me that I was lovable and helped me understand that God does indeed love me, too.

But this experience of love could come only after the healing I experienced through Sister Briege's ministry.

During the few months we were at *Our Sunday Visitor* in Indiana, I had read a book called *Catholic Pentecostals*. It was about that new wave of religious fervor beginning in the Catholic Church—and it claimed that people were being healed of all sorts of things, that people were being liberated from their own fears, set free to live happier and fuller lives.

I was very interested in this news. As a young boy in Louisiana, I was always intrigued by the stories of Jesus' miracles. And I often wondered, if the apostles could do the miracles reported in Acts, why couldn't the priest do miracles today? Was it not the same Church? The same God? The same Gospel?

I met Catholics who were excited about God, their faith, Catholics who spoke of Jesus as though he were really alive.

I was envious. Why hadn't God touched me in that way? Why was I still drinking to excess? Why didn't God wave his hand over me and make everything better?

There were stories of people suddenly finding their way out of debt, of people whose income suddenly seemed to stretch beyond reason to cover obligations, of people who were given new cars or had their old ones repaired free of charge. There were stories of people whose wayward children were suddenly converted.

Why them and not me?

There was a barrier inside me, something that kept me from giving myself completely to God. I believed in him, but I had not placed all my faith in him. I wanted to feel his healing touch, to learn to be fully a man, fully happy, fully able to cope, to relate well to others, to respect myself.

Nothing.

Pray. Pray. And pray again—and nothing.

I grew angry with God.

And then, in the summer of 1976, Sharon Sutter, a St. Petersburg diocesan reporter for *The Florida Catholic*, wrote a feature on Sister Briege McKenna, the Tampa nun who had experienced a miraculous healing and who now had an international healing ministry.

Sister Briege had been healed at an ecumenical prayer meeting in Orlando. She had been suffering from crippling arthritis, was consigned to a wheelchair and she was miraculously healed.

Later, in prayer, Sister Briege was given the gift of healing.

The story Sharon wrote about the nun moved me deeply. It was a story about a simple faith in God, a God who loved and who wanted his people healed both spiritually and physically.

I acknowledged the agony I had created for myself and I wanted to be healed.

I wrote Sister Briege.

I told her about the barrier, the pain, the desire to be freed from The Middle, to know and love God with all my heart.

She wrote back immediately, promising to pray for me.

"Pray?" I thought. "Pray? Where's the miracle? Why can't she heal me like the others?"

A few days later, still thinking of her ministry, and knowing that she often prayed with people by telephone and many were healed, I called her.

We talked for a while. She said the Lord would heal if only I had faith, and she said a prayer.

I began calling her on a regular basis—and she kept taking the calls. Today, all of us realize that God was bringing Briege, Peg and me together for a future work. Then, all I knew was that through this marvelous Christian minister I was finding new hope.

As a layman I frequently preached at weekend Masses in support of the Catholic press. I was scheduled to preach on October 30-31, 1976, at Corpus Christi Parish, Temple Terrace, near Tampa.

I called Briege and asked her to pray with me personally. She came to Corpus Christi Parish and prayed with me after the 10:30 Mass.

I had never met Briege personally. That morning, after the homily, I went into the parish social hall and Briege was waiting for me.

The pastor showed us into a private room.

We sat opposite each other in straightback chairs.

Sister Briege took my hands. I again told her I wanted to be able to give myself to God. I told her I had fasted and prayed that this would be the time and the place.

She began to pray. I remember much of her prayer verbatim. When God touches you, you remember.

It was as though a clear and bright light slowly flooded my mind and my heart.

Briege told me that as a first-grade teacher she used to try to teach her children the meaning of trust.

"I used to put them on a chair facing away from me. I'd tell them to shut their eyes and fall backwards into my arms—and they wouldn't do it. They were afraid. Even though I loved them, hugged and kissed them every day, they could not trust me.

"Henry, how hard it must be for you to trust a God you have not seen."

And she began to pray.

She prayed for Peg and me and for our marriage. She asked God to come to me in a special way. She asked Our Lady to intercede. She asked the Lord to give me the "beautiful gift of prayer."

Then it happened.

She continued to pray—and when she prays, Sister Briege gets images, insights, visions, call them what you will, that have a tremendous impact on people.

As she prayed with me, she said, "Henry, I see you all alone . . . [and I remember saying to myself, 'That figures; no one loves me.']

. . . and the Lord is with you and he is in the image of the Sacred Heart and his arm is around you. And he is saying, 'My son, that child of yours that you and your wife are praying so hard for, don't worry about him, my arm is around him and he's all right."

I began to weep with great, racking sobs. I had not told Sister Briege about our son who was going through a serious crisis, our son who had been so unhappy for so many years and now saw his dreams of love crumbling around him.

I knew that this was the Lord speaking to me. And he was saying, in effect, "Henry, I really know you. I know how you hurt. I love you. Trust me."

As I wept and tears rolled down my face, Sister Briege continued to pray. After a while she said, "I see you alone with the Lord again. His arm is around you. He is saying, 'My son, that member of your family who turned his back on you and the Church, who hurt your family so much, don't worry about him. My arm is around him and he's all right."

Again, I had not told Briege about this person, this pain, this hurt. It was the Lord, telling me again that he understands, knows and cares.

She prayed some more. Prayers of praise. Prayers of healing. And she had one more "word" from the Lord for me.

"Henry, as we pray, I see you on a mountaintop—and the Lord is with you. On the side of the mountain are many, many people. They're all looking up to the mountaintop and they want to be there. They see you there with the Lord and they want to be with the Lord, too, but they are afraid. They feel like social outcasts, like people in the Bible who suffered from leprosy—and they run into the rocks and shadows and hide.

"Henry, the Lord is calling you to a great work."

I really don't know how I preached the noon Mass. I was empty and full; drained and filled with strength; completely innocent and filled with understanding; as old as the ages and newborn.

I did preach that final Mass, somehow got my car on I-4 back to Orlando—and then I started singing, shouting and screaming. I couldn't keep my mouth shut or my hands and feet still. I sang. I prayed. I rolled down the window and stuck my head out and shouted as loudly as I could over and over again: "Jesus! It's true! It's true! Jesus! Jesus! It's true!"

And it is!

Peg and I were going to a Halloween party that night. Only about seven or eight close friends would be there.

I was so full of my experience I wanted to tell Peg about it. But I had never been able to share my spiritual side with her. Looking back, I suppose it was guilt and fear of rejection. "Why should she believe me? She knows I drink. She knows all my weaknesses. She won't believe me."

But driving to our friend's home that evening, I said, "Honey, I have something to tell you."

She stiffened, just a little. I suppose she was saying to herself, "Now what!"

I told her the story.

When I finished the story, telling her how I had sung and shouted all the way home, she reached over, put her hand on mine and said, "Honey, that's wonderful."

And it was!

That moment was a great breakthrough. Had Peg rejected my story, had she disbelieved me, I am not sure I would have had the strength to continue to believe that God had indeed touched me, healed me, promised me a role in his saving mission through his Church.

God used Peg to confirm my healing, my calling. It would be an ongoing confirmation and healing. Her love for me, her steadfastness, her loyalty and support are God's presence to me.

I hope, I pray that I am at least half as much a blessing to her as she is to me.

My sharing with her was the way God chose to make her part of it all. Briege had prayed for both of us, for our marriage, our love, our children, our ministry.

I know for sure that after all these ten years, my experience with the Lord through Sister Briege's ministry was *our* experience.

I can no longer see that moment without seeing Peg being physically present to it.

Looking back on that healing experience with Briege and then with Peg, I now realize that before I could be "delivered" from being caught in the middle between hope and despair, I had to admit my sin and brokenness. Then I had to desire to be forgiven and healed by God.

People don't want to admit their sins. They believe that if they deny them, God won't see them.

If you admit sin, then you have to admit that God is real, sees you, knows you. And when you first acknowledge God and recognize your own sins, you very likely will develop an unhealthy fear of God.

You begin to feel like a bug under a magnifying glass. You imagine, too, a huge fly swatter hovering expectantly over you, and you want to run, to hide from God, to deny your sin and therefore the reality of God.

In the Gospels, we read that a group of prominent citizens caught a woman in the very act of adultery. They took the woman and made her stand in front of a large crowd and they asked Jesus what to do about her.

Jesus was caught in the middle. If he showed mercy and said to release her, they would claim he was preaching against the holy law of Moses. If Jesus said they should follow the law and stone the woman, he would be denying his own Gospel of mercy and love.

We all know the story from John 8. Jesus wrote in the sand and, one by one, the woman's accusers left. But there is one very interesting line in the story. It says that after the accusers left, the woman "just stood there."

If I had been accused of a capital offense and my accusers ran off in one direction, I would have run off in another. But this woman "just stood there."

Perhaps, in her heart, she correctly sensed that there was someone present who was without sin and could cast the first stone. Perhaps she realized that Jesus was indeed her judge; so she just stood there, caught in the middle, fear and despair on the one hand, goodness and mercy on the other.

And because she did not run, she heard the verdict that Jesus wants to pronounce over each sinner, "I will not condemn you. Go in peace and commit this sin no more."

When I finally admitted my brokenness, when I finally prayed and fasted for deliverance from The Middle in which I saw only darkness and shadows of God's light, I discovered that God was present in my agony.

That is the beautiful thing about prayer. When a person at last touches the Lord, sees the Lord with the eyes of the heart, then prayer is itself an experience of deliverance from The Middle, even if we remain in The Middle. Faithful and trusting prayer changes circumstances. Sometimes circumstances are changed best when a person's perspective is broadened to embrace a greater wisdom within the pain and suffering.

Some people do not pray faithfully and with trust. Instead they pray as I did for many years: they throw their prayers heavenward and say, "If you're really there, catch this."

Prayer before conversion is really, truly prayer—but it brings little peace because it is aimed outward, upward. God is still "out there" and kept out there by the person's inability to see him within and in the present moment.

But when God, in his generosity, answers our hesitant hearts and reveals himself to us, we are surprised and thrilled to find him with us, in us, for us.

Often people ask, "What is the best way to pray?" Mother Angelica has a delightful pat answer, "The best way to pray is the way you pray best."

When we talk to one another we use our normal vocabulary and language. We don't concoct new phrases and flowery sentences. It should be the same with God. He understands all languages because he doesn't have ears. He is spirit. He reads other spirits—yours and mine, from within us.

One more important thing about The Middle is this: you cannot ignore it, wish it away or pretend it does not exist. To lie to yourself about The Middle is to stunt growth, beg mental and emotional problems, invite despair, make happiness impossible and alienate other people. Life is full of problems. That's a given. But life is full of answers to those problems, if only we are realistic enough to admit we have problems, name those problems, face them prayerfully and in faith.

Never try to cope with The Middle alone. I mean that you should depend on God, to be sure, but depend on others, too. God most often speaks to us through others—a husband or wife, a pastor or other friend. I have known so many people who go through life miserable, caught in the middle, and too proud or too shy or too private to share their grief with another human being. And this is pitiful—for naming the problem, telling it to another gives us power over the problems. As long as the problem is too big to be named, it is too big to be faced; too big to be faced, it is too big to be solved.

And that, really, is one of the big advantages Catholics have in the Sacrament of Reconciliation. By tradition, they are encouraged to name their problems, to seek elsewhere for solutions—they turn to God and to another human being. I'll return to this sacrament later.

After Sister Briege prayed with me, I grew excited about God, about life, about the Church and about the Bible. I read the Bible all the way through one year.

I finally was healed of alcoholism in September of 1977 (more on this later). It is important to realize that while prayer is always heard, sometimes God answers in ways we don't expect. Sometimes we don't want the answer he gives.

But it is important to remember that God is God and not us. I tire rapidly of the patter of certain Christians who "claim healings," and insist that you must "be specific" in your prayers because, if you don't, God presumably can't figure out how to answer your prayers. I tire of hearing people bombard the Father with the "name of Jesus," as though the name of Jesus were some magical key to God's treasury at heaven's North Pole.

I believe in praying in the name of Jesus—but when the Lord asks us to pray in his name, he is asking us to pray in his spirit, not just to use his name. The "name" of someone in the Old Testament times was synonymous with the person himself or herself. So to pray in the name of Jesus is to pray in harmony with, in tune with, in the spirit of, in the truth of, in the obedience of, in the love of, in the ministry of, in the service of Jesus. It is to be so close to Jesus, so united with him, that our prayer blends with his perfect prayer and the Father hears our petitions in the voice of Jesus.

But no, so many public Christians do not believe in this sort of prayer. It doesn't guarantee them the answers they want. Rather, they would insist that you must put in the right combination of words and scripture claims to force God to answer your prayer because he said he would and God is no liar. Amen? Amen! Alleluia? Alleluia!

The only good this kind of prayer accomplishes, if it is good, is to line the preacher's pocket. It focuses attention on the minister, not on the Lord. Oh, God can and does answer those kinds of prayers —but I like to think it's out of boredom and frustration rather than pleasure!

Don't ever let anyone tell you they have the secret to getting your prayers answered. They don't. They are not God and do not have a monopoly on God's attention, power or goodness.

And besides, there is no "secret" to getting prayers answered. You simply ask, and ask humbly, as a good child would ask, not whining or stomping feet or bargaining. Simply ask in love and tell the Lord you will accept whatever answer he has for you. That's praying in faith! You don't pray in faith when you demand of God a specific answer in a specific time frame. That's not faith; that's arrogance and belligerence. It's okay to say, "Lord, I sure need this money by Tuesday," as long as the Lord reads in your heart the fullness of the prayer of Jesus: "Your will, not mine, be done! I am willing, Lord, to lose my car if that is what you want. I can't see that, Lord, but if it happens, I will accept it as coming from your loving and generous hand." God often permits the unpleasant to give us a greater good than we asked for in the first place.

For example, I asked God for a new car. I couldn't afford one. The raises I prayed for and begged for did not come as I expected. One day, at prayer, I realized I was being very ungrateful. At least I did have a car. It ran fairly well. It was eight years old and had one hundred thousand miles and was beginning to need repairs. I realized I had to thank God for my car—and I did. Then I realized that my pay check comes from his providence. So I began to thank him for that pay check. He provides it even though I earn it—because I earn it with his gifts and in the job he provides. Yes, I truly believe God answers prayer, that he is concerned about our cars, jobs, kids, health and relationships.

But if there is any "secret" to prayer, it is this: Prayer is supposed to focus our attention on God rather than focus God's attention on us. His attention is already focused on us—it has always been and will always be focused on us, twenty-four hours a day and for all eternity! He knows our needs even before we utter them! (Rom. 8: 26ff., Ps. 139, Matt. 6:8).

With such love from God, the perfect prayer is that of Jesus in Gethsemane: "Thy will be done!"

Why are certain TV "healers" and "evangelists" so afraid of urging people simply to pray the prayer of Jesus, "Thy will be done." Oh, sure, Jesus did say, "Give us our daily bread," but he wasn't using 1970s and 80s jargon; he wasn't talking about cash and he wasn't talking only about food. He meant, give us today, the strength we need to remain faithful to you, our Father. Give us what we need to make your Kingdom come, to see that your will is done. That's praying in faith. With the fullness of tradition behind us, we look back into that prayer of Jesus to our Father and we know that he is telling us to pray for the fullness of the Spirit, that Spirit who will transform us in baptism and come to us in such personal ways to help us grow in the presence and love of God.

We don't need these televangelists who propagate false hope while they hold out their hands for our cash. Did you ever notice how many emergencies these people have? One might wonder whether they are indeed doing God's work or are they only working for God! To work for God is to do your own thing, presuming it pleases the Lord. To do God's work is to rely on him not only for inspiration but also for what is needed for the ministry.

That's how Sister Briege and Mother Angelica have put so many televangelists to shame. I've never heard Sister Briege ask for money for her international ministry. And Mother Angelica has a going network with a fraction of the staff the big networks have, with only two or three telethons in five years. She has faith. She did not aspire to television. Who had ever heard of a bunch of cloistered nuns running a TV network? No one had—until this great woman responded in faith to the Lord's call.

Notice God's sense of humor. The U.S. bishops had been talking for several years about needing to get a Catholic TV ministry started in this country. They talked and they talked. They did cost studies (or had them done) and everyone apparently shook his head over the huge sums of money it would take to establish Catholic TV in the U.S.

And along comes a little nun, in her sixties, with a back brace, no great theological or communications degrees. All she had was a life of prayer and the habit of saying "Yes" to the Lord, the habit of "being willing to do the ridiculous so God can do the miraculous." What is more ridiculous than that such a nun, with only $200 in the bank and eleven Sisters engaged in prayer, should establish the world's first Catholic satellite TV network?

But that's how God has worked so often throughout history. He doesn't need the fancy folks. He uses the simple to confound the wise. And he does so brilliantly.

The greatest evil perpetrated by certain televangelists is that they preach an incomplete Gospel. They forget the Cross.

They forget that in Gethsemane, Jesus begged the Father to let him escape the Passion. But the Father said, "No." Is it possible that Jesus didn't pray in faith? Didn't he know enough to ask for what he wanted in his own name? Could it be that he was not specific enough in prayer?

God is God. Not us. We do not make demands on God. The Christian stance is submission, with outstretched arms waiting for death or deliverance, knowing that the loving Father will be in both —and where he is there can be no despair or defeat.

Mother Angelica often complains that so many Christians fail to see beyond salvation. "After salvation, what?" And she answers her own question, "Spiritual growth."

Mother Angelica is a most fascinating person, an evangelizer and TV personality, a contemplative nun, an obedient Christian who makes liars out of people who say God's will cannot be done.

She has given the post-Vatican II Church a great gift—an example of how central prayer is to successful ministry, of how spiritual growth is possible only through prayer and order in the Christian community.

In a very real sense, Mother Angelica has given the Christian Church in the U.S. its first real look in a long, long time at the full Gospel of Jesus Christ, a Gospel that contains Word and work, personal relationships with Jesus and the reality of the Church, with its authority, variety, complexity and simplicity.

What a grand lady she is! In the next chapter, I want to share how she affected me and my spiritual growth. What I learned from her may help you or someone you know.

Chapter 2

THE MINISTRY OF MOTHER ANGELICA

I once had the pleasure of introducing Mother Angelica to a congregation of more than one thousand people.

The people exploded with laughter when I said, "I met Mother Angelica in a motel room and her first words to me were, 'Hi, Honey!'"

And that's the truth.

Father David Page, my executive editor who is also pastor of St. James Cathedral Parish in Orlando, had invited Mother to preach at all Masses one weekend. He also suggested that I interview her.

Since there was no convent in the parish, Mother Angelica and the Sister who traveled with her were lodged in a respectable motel near the parish church.

I remember walking up to the motel door as though it were the entrance to the gas chamber.

I muttered and swore under my breath, calling down all kinds of Cajun "blessings" on Father Page's head. "A nun! A nun who writes books—and the dingbat GIVES them away! About what they're worth, I guess!"

I lugged a camera case with me, a notebook stuck into my pants.

I knocked on the door. A youngish nun opened it wide and swung away from me as it opened—and there stood Angelica, with her arms wide open, a huge grin on her impish face and she said with warm delight, "Hi, Honey!"

That did it! I became her friend immediately.

From that moment, Mother Angelica had my total attention—and my heart.

As she told me her story of faith, of total dependency on God, of trusting God to live up to his promises, I began to sense a deep excitement. There seemed to be an inner voice saying, "Okay, Henry. You wanted it; now you're gonna get it!"

When we parted, she, too, prayed with me.

I'll never forget that prayer.

It was a prayer for the gifts of the Spirit.

Sister Briege had prayed for the beautiful gift of prayer.

Mother Angelica now prayed for the fullness of the Spirit, for the awakening of the gifts that come with baptism, those transforming gifts that are listed in Isaiah 11:1 and following.

The power of that prayer demands that it be shared. I offer it here.

"Lord Spirit, I pray that you give Henry the gift of Fear of the Lord. Lord, let him stand in awe of you. Let him see you as his Father, himself as creature and you as loving Creator.

"Lord, please give Henry the gift of Piety. Lord, put in his heart an intense love for you and for his brothers and sisters. Let him see, Lord, that if you are Father to all, he is brother to all. Give him, Lord Spirit, the gift of right relationship.

"Lord, I pray that you will give Henry the gift of Fortitude. Grant, Lord, that he has the courage to share his faith with his family and friends and to do your will in all situations. Give him strength to resist temptation by flying to you in time of need.

"I ask you, Lord God, to give this man the gift of Counsel. Lord, help him recollect your Word as he needs it in every situation in life. When he is counseling his children, or friends or writing in the paper, dear God, give him a clear understanding of your Word and your will, of the teachings of your Church. Help him love your Word and to seek you in scripture.

"Jesus, I pray that you will send your Spirit upon Henry with the gift of Knowledge. Lord Spirit, help him to realize that only one thing counts—the glory of the Father and the good of his neighbor. Help him see that the two are one, that you cannot glorify the Father if you ignore your neighbor and you cannot help your neighbor without glorifying the Father.

"I pray, too, Lord Spirit, that you give him the gift of Understanding. Help him understand that the Father loves him as much as he loves Jesus, that if Henry were the only person in the world, the Father would send Jesus to die for Henry alone.

"And Lord, I ask that you send upon Henry your Spirit of Wisdom that he might become, Lord, one with you, that like St. Paul he may be so full of Christ that it is Christ who lives in him, that he becomes, through your indwelling power, whom he worships, so one with you, Lord, that when people look upon Henry they see you and are called to you.

"We pray this, Father, in the name of Jesus."

I was moved deeply by this prayer. Sister Briege had prayed for me only two weeks earlier. I was still sailing high, still feeling the warmth of the Lord's healing love—and Mother Angelica's prayer, which was also an instruction in the life of the Spirit, centered my attention on union with God instead of only receiving his favors.

When the Lord heals, he is calling people to himself. When he does not heal, he is still calling people to himself.

Mother Angelica's kindness and patience over several years helped me develop a keener sense of the importance of *the present moment*.

People live in the past, or they live in the future, or they try to escape the present in other ways, such as drinking and other forms of addiction.

But *the present moment*, perhaps another real good name for The Middle, is where creature and Creator meet, converse and relate.

Christians try to escape the present moment when there is pain —and they do not, of course, want pain; or when they are unemployed; or when their unmarried daughter announces, "I'm pregnant."

By the grace of the Holy Spirit, that wonderful Counselor who is so much ignored and so little adored, Christians are empowered to live in the present moment.

The Holy Spirit gives us the seven gifts mentioned in Mother's prayer—Fear of the Lord, Piety, Fortitude, Counsel, Knowledge, Understanding and Wisdom. These gifts, through his presence in us, with Jesus and the Father, carry us through each and every moment of our lives.

There are many people, some of them priests, and even a few unsympathetic bishops, who seem to think Mother Angelica is some sort of spiritual simpleton whose lack of theological sophistication discredits her as a Catholic evangelist.

To the contrary, I have seen and experienced personally the freeing power of her ministry. She stands for truth, for the Gospel, for the teachings of the Church—and she speaks to the hearts of people because she looks into the heart of Jesus rather than only into cumbersome theology books.

Once, when she was having a great deal of bad press from certain officials in the Catholic communications and a few bishops were really "on her case," I called five bishops to tell them I thought she deserved better treatment.

One of those bishops decided to fly to Birmingham and see her for himself. Today he is a cardinal! See there!

Mother Angelica's keen sense of God's presence and her uncanny ability to get to the heart of the matter have made her one of the most effective teachers in the Church today.

She is master of moods, can woo audiences and have them in deep reflection one moment and, with her saucy humor, have them rolling in the aisles the next.

I've experienced the "many faces of Angelica."

One day I phoned her to complain about how stubborn one of my daughters was being. I was looking for a prayer and sympathy —mostly sympathy, I suppose.

But Mother had a different idea. She said, "Henry, do you think you and your daughter have trouble getting along because you're so much alike?"

I laughed good naturedly and said, "Yes, that's probably it," thinking admission of guilt would get me off the hook.

But not with this nun who likes to see editors squirm. She shot back, "Then, its like one jackass talking to another, isn't it!"

We both had a good, genuine laugh. The truth will set you free, even when it pinches the ego a little.

Her spirituality attracted me, led me into more frequent and deeper prayer. I devoured all her tracts and the bigger books, too.

I liked especially *I Am His Temple*, her book on the gifts of the Spirit. Her prayer for me, the day we met, echoes this book. I've read it time and again.

And the one on the beatitudes as well, *In His Sandals*.

She later gave me a larger book (now out of print) called *Three Keys to the Kingdom*. She and I still laugh over my experience with that book. I thought it was the dullest thing I had ever read—but something said, "Keep reading." I would manage to read one or two pages before going to sleep out of sheer boredom. Finally, I finished the book.

But was I falling asleep only out of boredom? If so, how could I have awakened one day with the contents of the book so clear in my mind? I could teach the book's contents—that book I had found so boring—with clarity and conviction. I was excited about the makeup of the soul—memory, intellect, will; excited, too, about how the virtues of faith, hope and love nurtured the soul. It was an insight into how God works in the human soul. I remember how excited I was with human anatomy in my college studies; now I was excited about "soul anatomy"!

Little did I realize at that time that I had mastered a lesson that would carry me through ten years of preaching and teaching and pave the way for Peg and me in ministry.

Because of the inspiration I received from that book and others written by Mother Angelica, I was able to write 180 one-minute radio spots without extensive rewrite except on about ten of them. I recorded most of them on the first try (except number twenty, which took twenty-six tries before I got it right!). I became known around the radio station as "one-shot Henry."

I launched a successful prison ministry. Over the following years I was invited to preach in some sixty parishes in Florida.

No, I wasn't falling asleep out of boredom when I struggled with *Three Keys to the Kingdom*. I believe now that often when I slept, I was "resting in the Spirit," was literally being lulled to sleep by the Lord so that he could minister to my mind and heart without self-created distractions.

After Sister Briege and Mother Angelica, I spent long hours reading the scriptures and reading Mother Angelica's books. I received what Briege had prayed for, "the beautiful gift of prayer."

I spent a lot of money on long-distance phone calls to both of them, but since Sister Briege was out of the country a lot, I found myself drawn more and more to Mother Angelica and her spiritual direction.

Peg and I became involved in the now disbanded Catholic Family Missionary Alliance. Through that work of spreading the Good News through distribution of Mother Angelica's free tracts and through sharing her ministry in retreats and conferences, Peg and I finally became leaders of a small prayer group in the Orlando area, the Spirit of God Community.

We pray the Liturgy of the Hours and attend daily Mass (those who can), and we pray in community every Friday night, interceding for the Church. We pray especially for the pope, our own bishop and pastors and for all who are to preach in our diocese that weekend. And we pray for those who have to listen to sermons! We pray for the lectors, the servers, for those who will celebrate the liturgy, lead congregational singing, serve as eucharistic ministers and ministers of hospitality.

Through the spiritual support of the community, I began "Thought for Today," the one-minute spot I've already mentioned. It ran in morning drive-time on Christian station WAJL in Orlando. We alternated those 180 spots, which offered free tracts.

That program ran for about five years until Peg and I entered the Pastoral Ministries Program in the Orlando diocese on our way to the diaconate. I cancelled the program because the 180 spots had to be redone to accommodate a new mailing address and, with studies, I did not have time to redo them.

I was commissioned a pastoral minister and lay evangelist by Bishop Thomas J. Grady of Orlando, June 1, 1985. And on May 18, 1986, Pentecost Sunday, I was ordained to the diaconate.

The four years of training were filled with blessings: through the young-adult ministry in our parish, I learned more about one-on-one ministry. I came to grips with the differences between evangelization and catechesis, with the justice issues in the Church (women, minorities, poverty, war and peace). During those four years, I earned sixty-four credits to finish my B.A. in religious studies and another twenty-six credits for my M.A. in pastoral ministry from St. Thomas University, Miami.

Peg and I grew closer together through the shared-study and community-formation experience.

As I prayed and reflected on ordination, two central themes rose to the surface, themes born of Briege's ministry to me that Halloween day and throughout the following ten years and born, too, of Mother Angelica's spiritual direction.

One theme is "grateful repentance." The other, "servant love." Both are passwords to meeting God in The Middle of any life situation. They have become for me two pillars of wisdom. Because we are in constant conversion, in constant need to repent and to become reconciled with God and one another, we should always have a repentant spirit. And realizing that salvation is a free gift, that we can't and don't need to earn it, that God-is-with-us in love, we experience a sense of profound gratitude. These two, repentance and gratitude, come to us together. So I have called them "grateful repentance."

Servant love. Now that's a "biggy." It came to me as I was writing in my journal one night. It was April 1, 1986. Shortly after 9:30 P.M. I was writing as I "spoke" to the Lord, "mourning" the passing of *The Catholic Evangelist* magazine, which I had published for ten short months, hoping to save it, hoping to expand my ministry to a broader audience.

I hadn't been giving God the full hour of prayer each day that I had promised. I was in the midst of preparations for ordination to the diaconate. We had been going through some very serious discussions concerning employee salaries and benefits at *The Florida Catholic*. There was a lot of pressure on Peg and me at that time.

I was begging the Lord for the strength to say "Yes" in any and all situations. And in my "conversation" with the Lord, this is, in part, what I "heard" as I wrote in my journal:

"There must be a new power in my Church. A power of servant love. I want my priests, deacons and bishops and my sisters and brothers, and all my lay ministers, to be filled with servant love . . .

"Servant love is a special gift from my Spirit—a gift that enables my chosen servants to see me in all people and in each person.

"Until you see me even in those you despise the most, you do not have servant love.

"Servant love is the love of my servant for me; it is the love of service to others, in my name; it is me living and ministering in you, living fully as you die to self. How I want to reach my people! I can do it only through my loving servants. If you do not die to self, if you place your own desires and ideas and notions first, if you serve yourself and not others, I cannot speak to my people . . .

"You must increase in servant love for your enemies . . . I want you to give servant love to those who hurt you. I will use you to heal them and call them into full reconciliation and give them great fruits in their ministry. They are broken, my son, but they do not feel as loved as you do. Love them for me and with me . . ."

I wouldn't share so much of this here, except that, after sharing it with the Spirit of God Community, I am convinced the Lord intends his message about servant love to be shared by the broader Church.

How do you love and forgive people who have hurt you deeply, people who have, through a lie, dashed your ministerial dreams to the earth? How can you forgive children, parents, co-workers, bosses? How can you love them enough to forgive them?

The next chapter will deal with forgiveness. I am convinced that most people find it hard to forgive. And they suffer because of it. It is agonizing to be caught in the middle between a subtle but strong thirst for revenge and the demands of the Gospel to forgive and forget.

Servant love is living as Jesus lived. He died for love of all humankind. He died for his enemies. That is his Way. We claim to love him and serve him. Yet, we are selective in accepting his Way. We want to experience healings and love, we want to be forgiven, but we do not want to die for others as Jesus did.

To love Jesus with one's whole heart and soul is to give up one's right to justice and fair treatment. Nothing was just or fair about the Cross. The Cross is the ultimate statement Jesus makes about love, about his Way, about how he calls people to himself. "And I —once I am lifted up from the earth—will draw all men to myself" (John 12:32).

Grateful repentance and servant love are the golden threads that hold together the tapestry of Matthew 5, 6 and 7, the basic message of Jesus' ministry, a message of forgiveness and praise and worship, of healing and love.

Grateful repentance and servant love are the pillars of the Beatitudes, the foundation of the Lord's Prayer, the goal and message of good liturgy, and the heart of missionary outreach.

They are the way to cope with any sort of Middle. Through grateful repentance and servant love, parents gain strength to face disappointments in their children, children can make sense of the weaknesses of their parents, pastors can cope with the discouragement of apathetic parishioners, young adults can find strength in their loneliness and restlessness.

Grateful repentance and servant love are in The Middle for God is there, and these are two of the special gifts of his Spirit.

If I were to synopsize what I learned from Sister Briege and Mother Angelica, I would simply state, "grateful repentance and servant love."

It was in my prayer with Sister Briege that I found how great a joy it is to turn to the Lord with all your heart and soul, without reservation, in total surrender, with deep gratitude.

And it was in Mother Angelica's spiritual direction over several years, as well as in my private prayer as I prepared for ordination, that the importance of forgiveness took root in me, paving the way for the Lord to teach me about servant love.

Don't be afraid of the Lord, of letting him see you as you are— because he already does see you as you are. He hasn't killed you or swatted you with that big fly swatter. No. He looks at you and loves you.

Stand before the Lord. In the next chapter and in those that follow, measure your Middle with that of others treated in this book. Let the Lord speak to you as he lives in you and shares (yes, he shares your pain and anxieties!) in your Middle.

Chapter 3

THE POWER OF FORGIVENESS

A Tampa man drove across Florida to visit a convicted murderer in Florida State Prison. When he arrived, he was unable to see the man; so he left a written message with the chaplain.

When the young convict opened the letter, this is basically what he read:

"Dear Joe, my wife and I forgive you for murdering our son. We want to be your friends and to help you if we can."

The letter was signed and had a return address.

The parents of the murdered boy and the murderer became friends. Through this Christian couple, the young murderer found new life. He experienced firsthand the forgiving love of God.

Forgiving is never easy. In the minds of most people to forgive is stupid, weak. But I am convinced that in forgiving we are most perfectly, if ever, fools for Christ.

Forgiveness is the key to freedom when we are caught in the middle between anger and love.

I have trouble forgiving. I am strong, proud, even arrogant. When I am right, I am right. I also have a degree of wisdom. I discern well. I know right from wrong. I am a prophet by nature and, I believe, by calling as well.

When my grown children began making decisions that I was convinced were wrong, I grew very angry and resentful. I love my children and they know it. Although they are all grown, I hug them

33

all—men and women alike. They are my children. I embrace them.

But I can be angry and unfriendly when offended. For several years, I held some of my children on emotional tenterhooks, always letting them know by frown or wisecrack that I thought they were in error if not in actual sin.

One weekend during our pastoral ministries training, in January, 1985, Jim Luntz, a dear friend and classmate, pounded on the door to our room at 3 A.M.

Their nineteen-year-old son had just been killed in an accident.

I spent most of the day with the family. Peg stayed on at the weekend.

On Saturday night, I returned to the retreat and my class was meeting in small groups. Everyone was terribly sad. In November, one of our classmates had died suddenly the day after we buried a mutual friend, Peg Ward—and Peg's husband, Deacon Bud Ward, had only a couple of months to live. It was a sad Saturday evening.

After dinner, we had a healing service.

We had a scripture reading and homily and then we broke up into our care groups. I was still very sad—and somewhat stunned. During that entire day, I kept thinking, "If it had been one of my children, he would have died with me mad at him."

In our care groups we were supposed to share whatever was on our minds. I blurted out, "I have to do something about this anger I have toward my kids."

The group was fantastic. Viv Grenon, the widow of our deceased classmate, has deep insight and a gentle way of helping people through trying times. She ministered to me that night. I made a resolution to forgive my children.

We were anointed with oil and then we all went to bed.

About four the next morning, I found myself suddenly wide awake with a desire to pray before the Blessed Sacrament. The chapel was just around the corner from my room, so I dressed as quietly as I could and let myself out of the room. Peg was still sleeping.

As I walked into the chapel, I saw two chairs side by side before the tabernacle. I sat in one.

I began to pray the morning prayer in the Liturgy of the Hours.

When I finished, I began to reflect on my relationship with the children.

Here, I will not name my children. But I did name them one by one to the Lord, saying, "Lord I give you (name), and I give you (her/his) problem. Lord, I know you love them and I know you can help them. I give this matter completely over to you." One by one I prayed this prayer for all my children. When I named one of them with whom I was especially angry, I would cry a little harder, until at the end of this "giving prayer" I was weeping audibly.

After weeping and having gotten rid of the problem, I felt much better.

Jesus, however, was not finished with me.

"Henry," I distinctly heard him say in my spirit, "thank you for giving them to me. Now you must forgive them."

I felt as though a heavy weight had descended on me. My anger boiled up. But I knew it was the Lord; so, still weeping, I began to name each of my adult children saying, "Lord, I forgive (name)."

When it came to two of them in particular, I had great difficulty naming them. It was as though the word "forgive" stuck in my throat, smothered me, promised to kill me if I spoke it. It required great physical and spiritual strength to name those two children in a "forgiving prayer." So deep was my hurt. So deep my anger. So deep my love—love which, I now realize, I considered had been rejected.

But I did speak the names in the forgiving prayer—and when all seven had been named and forgiven, I wept because of the joy the Lord gave me.

Perhaps this was my first conscious experience of the joy that lies beyond forgiveness. I asked God to forgive me for my anger and resentment toward my own children. I had concentrated on my hurt rather than on their needs. I could not see beyond the pain. I had lashed out in fury instead of forgiving in love.

No, forgiving isn't easy.

When you forgive, you give up your right to justice, to restitution. You say to those who hurt you, "I don't count. You do. I want you to have the peace of being forgiven." When you forgive, you are like Jesus—you die so others may live.

I am convinced that forgiveness is the greatest act of love. People look to the Crucified One and see a dead body, a body that would rise again. But on the Cross, Jesus still had a choice to make—to forgive or to condemn. His physical death was not enough. He had to die to self, had to forego the right to justice, to restitution, had to choose between total gift of self in forgiveness or a mere physical death that, in all probability, would have fallen short of redemption.

Jesus chose to forgive.

We can do no less if we are truly serious about transcending The Middle and becoming followers of Jesus, Christians in fact as well as in name.

I am also convinced that many people find it impossible to forgive because they have not felt God's forgiveness. They have not felt God's forgiveness because they have never asked—or because they have never forgiven themselves.

In the Sermon on the Mount, Jesus tells us that if we don't forgive others, we cannot be forgiven. I believe that goes for ourselves, too. If we don't forgive ourselves or others, we do not understand forgiveness—and if we do not understand it, we cannot truly desire it.

To understand forgiveness requires a lot of reflection. Forgiveness, when it comes from the Lord, always means reconciliation. If a person is looking for absolution without relationship, then forgiveness cannot come. For absolution is rooted in relationship, not directed toward isolated acts that offend a disembodied law or command. God *is* his word, his law, his command.

To offend God is to insult him personally, not merely break one of his rules. The rules tell us who he is more than what he wants. The Commandments, true enough, tell us what God wants—but he wants more from people than adherence to Commandments. The Commandments are part of his I.D., part of who he is. Obeying the Commandments comes from knowing him and loving him. Otherwise, we border on idolatry even in obeying God's Commandments. In this sense, we understand better St. Paul who said that once he was saved by justification through faith in Jesus, he was above the law (Gal. 2:16-21). To be one with Jesus is to be at the heart of the law, not on the outside looking in.

To forgive myself, which took a long, long time, I had to understand how much Jesus loved me—and in him, how much the Father loved me.

I had many sins that shamed me. And the shame was sinful in itself because I was more conscious of my own wounded pride than I was of my offended God. I had a quick temper, a sometimes violent nature. I was addicted to alcohol and nicotine. I had little self-respect. I had always had trouble with my own sexuality and, with no healthy sex education, had brought to our marriage what I had learned in the gutter, so to speak.

Confessor after confessor, director after director would tell me things like, "Don't take yourself so seriously," or "The Lord understands and he loves you just as you are."

I knew in my head they were right, but in my heart I lived in fear of God. After Sister Briege's prayer and Mother Angelica's direction, things became much better. But I still had a tremendous hang-up about my sins.

I want to share an experience I had with one of my spiritual directors before returning to this subject of forgiving oneself. The story makes a pertinent point.

A Franciscan priest, Father Bonaventure Midilli, TOR, was in the Orlando diocese for a time. He served as my spiritual director for a couple of years. Bonny used to frustrate me almost to tears. All he did for two years was ask, "Why?"

How I hated that question!

I had been coping with the realization that I, Henry Libersat, would die. Realizing you are going to die is a very sobering thought. I feared the process of dying, not being dead, because I believe in eternal life. But, *dying* means going where you would not, feeling yourself slip away and being unable to do anything about it, dying and not being able to choose the how, the why and the time. *Dying* means losing all control!

One day, I rushed into Bonny's office and flashed one of my "Ah-Hah!" Cajun grins. He asked why I was so happy. I said, "Because I have the perfect Christian definition of what it means to die!"

"Oh," he said with his slow smile, "and what is your definition of dying?"

"It's a *regrettable nuisance*," I said, beaming.

Bonny looked at me and kept right on smiling and asked, "Why?"

I was so frustrated that all I could do was sputter and try to change the subject—but Bonny is a good director and he would not let me off the hook.

Finally, the dawn! "It's a regrettable nuisance," I told him, "because I will have nothing to say about it, will have no control over it and that scares hell out of me."

"Now," he said, "we are getting somewhere."

And we were.

A Christian cannot understand death apart from her or his daily dying to self. If a Christian is not sacrificing time, talent and treasure, if a Christian is not dying the death of forgiving and servant love, that Christian cannot understand or accept death.

I grew very slowly in my understanding of repentance, of change of heart and the joy that can bring. I grew even more slowly in the spirit of forgiveness which, I believe, is synonymous with my theme of servant love.

One evening, at a healing Mass in St. Mary Magdalen Parish, a very good friend, Father Eamon Tobin, led us through a spiritual reflection after Communion. When I went into the church that night, I had no idea that I would have encountered the Lord in a way that would once and for all free me from unhealthy guilt and place in my heart a firm sense of grateful repentance.

That night, in my imagination, I was to encounter Jesus.

After Communion, Eamon asked us to go, in our imagination, each to his or her favorite prayer spot, to invite Jesus to come in and sit, to tell Jesus what each of us had on his or her mind.

That was easy for me. My favorite spot is our prayer room, a converted bedroom. The Word is enthroned on a simple altar in what was formerly a closet. There are three old church pews on the three other walls, two stands with busts of Mary and Francis, a candle near the Bible and other holy pictures, plus personal sacramentals such as pictures of Bob Grenon and Bud Ward.

So, in my imagination, I sat in my favorite spot and imagined Jesus coming into the room.

It was such a real experience that later I recorded it in my journal—and in recording it, lived it again for a double blessing. I have used this story with several groups and even in preaching at Sunday liturgies (in the latter case not identifying myself as the one who had the experience).

This is how the experience unfolded.

As I sat in church after Communion, I followed Eamon's directions. I imagined myself back in my prayer room, in my favorite spot.

After a moment, I saw Jesus stick his head through the door. He smiled warmly and just waited there, as though asking, "Is it okay if I come in?"

I smiled back, slapped the pew next to me and said, "Come in Jesus. Sit next to me."

And he did.

As he sat down, I sort of leaned over and we hugged each other tightly. Then I leaned my head on his chest. I could hear his heart thumping. We stayed that way for a while, his arm over my shoulders.

Then I sat back and said, "Jesus, I want to give myself to you completely. I give you my life, my home, my family, all my possessions. I give you my talents and all my strengths. I give you my joy. Please forgive me my sins. I love you so much."

And Jesus said, "Thank you, Henry. I love you, too."

We just sat there for a moment. Then after a while, he looked over at me. His eyes were so gentle, so good. He said, "Henry, give me your sins."

I was shocked.

"Oh, no! Oh, no, Lord! My sins are so dirty, so evil. You are so good, so holy. I could not give you my sins."

"Henry, give me your sins," he said more insistently.

Still, I refused.

Then Jesus held out his crucified hands, cupping them in front of me and said firmly, "Henry, give me your sins."

I began to cry and said, "Okay, Lord, if that's really what you want."

And I named each of my sins, one by one dropping them into the cupped, crucified hands of Jesus.

As I dropped my sins into his hands, I began to feel lighter, less worried about his seeing all my sins so openly—without darkness, without a priest standing between him and me, without veils or curtains or fancy language. Here was Jesus and me and my sins. Everything was out in the open—and he was touching my sins, touching me, and he didn't find it repulsive.

Finally, I finished—and I was really feeling great. The guilt was gone, the sins were gone. I noticed suddenly that my sins, in Jesus' hands, were covered by his blood.

Jesus held his hands out to me and said, "Now, take them back."

"Oh, no, Lord. I don't want them back. Here I am all cleaned up and not feeling dirty or guilty anymore and you want me to take them back? Oh, no, Lord. They're too dirty, too evil. I don't want them back."

He insisted, "Take them back, for this is who you are, Henry, a sinner covered with my blood."

I took them back—and was surprised to discover they still did not make me feel dirty or guilty.

It was a great lesson.

At that time, I heard Eamon's voice from the sanctuary calling us back to the present moment.

I went home that night fully forgiven, for I had at last forgiven myself.

People do not forgive themselves because they misunderstand God. If only people could hear God preached more lovingly and more personally by preachers. If only more preachers permitted the Lord to instruct them in what to say! If only people could be convinced that they are already forgiven, even before the asking, but that God doesn't force himself, not even his forgiveness, on anyone! If only people could realize that to know God is to love him, that to repent is to find fuller life, that to avoid evil pleasures (such as illicit sex or abuse of food or drink) is to find greater pleasure in freedom from addiction!

But we don't preach, very often, such a Gospel.

How I wish everyone in the world could think long and hard about that story of the woman taken in adultery in John 8. I urge you to read that Gospel, to reflect on how the woman, as I have said, "just stood there," how Jesus always forgives if we stick around to hear what he has to say, if we look at him nailed to the

Cross, if we see in the Cross the ultimate expression of his forgiving love.

The power of that passage is this: If we do not run away and hide from Jesus when we have sinned, if we stand before him humbly and honestly admitting sin, his sentence is always forgiveness!

We so often hear, "Don't just stand there, do something." In this case, we need to remember to "just stand there."

It does no good to run from Jesus. He already knows the sin. Running away just makes things worse. Running could be another sin, a lack of trust, a desire to lie to God, a resistance to his gentle call to repentance, a rejection of his outstretched, crucified hand.

I have told this story time and again. Always, people come to me afterward and thank me for it. There is liberation in faithful and faith-filled preaching of the Gospel. The truth, indeed, sets us free. This is the kind of preaching we need.

We need to recognize our own personal sinfulness, our own brokenness. Today, however, we are inclined to mistake social and political concerns for the central issue. We are negating sin and blaming everything on social evils, forgetting that the whole is equal to the sum of its parts, that if there are social evils it is only because there are enough individual evil people in the world to make society evil. If the Gospel were preached in power, the world could be turned around, the Church could become a revolutionary power —as was Jesus.

Jesus attacked sin, but he showed mercy. There is one very powerful, revealing and moving story about how Jesus responds to sin, to repentant sinners and to hypocritical sinners. It is in the Gospel according to Luke 7:36-50.

In this Gospel story, Jesus goes to the house of Simon, a Pharisee, for dinner. In those days, in the Holy Land, when a rabbi or some other important person visited a home, the host threw open his doors to the people of the community. Everyone had a right to come into the house, to see and hear the famous person.

This did a lot for the host's standing in the community and, in this case, Simon apparently was enjoying the attention brought to him through the presence of Jesus.

One of the people who came into Simon's home was a prostitute, a public sinner. The Gospel says that she approached Jesus' feet as he reclined at table to eat. She "stood behind him at his feet, weeping so that her tears fell upon his feet. Then she wiped them with her hair, kissing them and perfuming them with oil."

Simon thought to himself (my own paraphrase), "Some prophet this guy is! If he were a prophet he would know that this woman is a common slut and he wouldn't let her touch him."

But Jesus read Simon's thoughts and upbraided him for not extending the customary courtesies to himself when he entered the house. Then Jesus pointed to the woman and said something a little strange in the light of his saving grace. He said that "her many sins are forgiven—because of her great love." Does this mean the woman earned salvation? No. You cannot be saved by your works, and love is a work. The scriptures have a deeper meaning.

The woman approached Jesus fearfully. She must have been drawn toward him by some deep desire to be received, accepted, loved, forgiven. She must have seen in Jesus what we see—a God willing to forgive, eager to forgive.

I can just see her as she first arrived at Jesus' feet. She suddenly realized that Jesus did not draw away from her, did not recoil in disgust, did not accuse her publicly of her sin. As she leaned over to kiss his feet in loving gratitude for his forgiveness, such joy welled up in her heart that she burst out weeping. Her tears fell on his feet. She kissed his precious feet, those feet that would be pierced by nails for her sins, and yours, and mine.

She anointed his feet with perfume.

And she loved. She loved before she realized she was forgiven, but having felt Jesus' acceptance of her, as she was, a public sinner, she was grateful, and filled with joy, loved all the more. She developed a spirit of grateful repentance—and one of servant love.

It was grateful repentance that caused her to bend over Jesus' feet in servant love.

God's love and holiness draw sinners close; they realize they are acceptable to God and they accept forgiveness; forgiveness inspires gratitude and love that in turn, lead to repentance. Repentance leads a sinner to the highest form of love, to greater love, to servant love.

Jesus finally looked at her. He spoke those words that make a sinner's heart sing for joy: "Your sins are forgiven. Your faith has been your salvation. Go now in peace."

Christian pulpits must make Jesus' words come alive for sinners —and we all sin. We don't need another Bishop Sheen in every pulpit. We need committed, convinced and renewed preachers in every pulpit; preachers who believe with all their hearts; preachers who, themselves wounded by sin, have great compassion for sinners; preachers who, themselves touched by God, can promise the touch of God to others.

We don't need preachers with great oratorical skills, although preachers of faith who have talent are a joy. We need faithful, and faith-filled preaching, the kind of preaching that puts hope on Christians' faces and fire into their hearts.

As a Catholic I yearn for the day when more of our own preachers can "preach with power," can say with conviction, because they have experienced personally the Lord's mercy, "You are forgiven. Come, kneel before the feet of the Lord. Bathe his wounds with your tears. Show him your gratitude, your love. You have been set free! You are daughters and sons of the Father, sisters and brothers of Jesus, temples of the Holy Spirit. You have been transformed. You are a new creation, a city on a hill, a light shining in the darkness, a refuge for the lonely and the broken. You have the power of God. You are the link between heaven and earth, the continuing incarnation of Jesus, the spoken Word of the Father, the breath of the Spirit."

Oh, dear Lord, speed that day! Put the fire of faith and the pillar of hope into the hearts of your preachers and the pulpits of your churches!

God's people so often seem like sheep without a shepherd. They cry out for guidance, for truth. They get, too often, warmed over, pussyfooting platitudes. Some preachers are afraid to speak the truth. They are afraid to tell their lustful congregations that premarital sex is sinful, that adultery is sinful. They are afraid to tell their greedy and prejudiced congregations that abuse of employees is sinful, that injustice to women, minorities, the oppressed is sinful. There *is* such a thing as personal sin.

Jesus came to point out sin and to call people into repentance and forgiveness. He pointed to personal sin as well as social sin. There can be no social sin unless there is first personal sin. Society is the sum of its individual parts. You don't begin with society; you begin with individuals.

If public morals are bad, if there is injustice in the world it is because many, many individual people have bad morals and are unjust.

Only conversion of the heart will change the world—and "the world" doesn't have a heart. People do.

If Christian churches, and particularly the Catholic Church with its rich tradition of faith and holiness, would begin to preach powerfully the Gospel of forgiveness, the world could be changed.

But before people can seek forgiveness they must be convinced they are sinners. The churches are not telling them they are sinners. They are only broken. True, people are broken. But they have broken themselves. They have chosen sin over righteousness. They have chosen themselves over God. They have chosen fleeting pleasure over personal and social integrity, over God's gift of joy and eternal life.

The churches must help people realize they are in sin by choice. People have a free will. They make decisions about their conduct, values, relationships.

People do have a choice. "Everybody does it" is no excuse. Christians do not have to pay starvation wages or peddle drugs. They do not have to commit adultery or engage in premarital sex. Christians do not have to practice homosexuality or promote prostitution. They do not have to stay angry and spiteful or con people out of hard-earned cash, lie in business deals or cheat on tests.

Christians, if they are Christians, show people there is another Way, a better Way.

The churches—to liberate people from Satan—must help people admit they are sinners, that God does exist and that he wants his people to love him and serve him. The Church, if it is like Jesus, tells people they are sinners, not in a condemning way, but in the way Jesus told and tells people they are sinners. In the story of Simon and the prostitute, there are *four elements* in forgiveness.

First, there is the recognition of God's holiness. Jesus himself was holy. That's why the prostitute knew she was a sinner. She was not what Jesus was. She saw him, loved him for his holiness— and that is the heart of repentance, to love Jesus for his holiness.

Second, there is the conviction, the realization that "I am a sinner." Jesus helped people realize they were in sin. He tried to tell

Simon that he was in sin. "You did not show me courtesy or respect, Simon, when I entered your house. See, this woman is justified. She has accepted forgiveness. You, my poor, rich friend, are not even aware of your sin. How poor you really are, but how rich is this woman who is weeping over my feet and kissing them."

Third, the sinner recognizes and consciously receives the gift of forgiveness. Jesus told the woman, "Your sins are forgiven. Your faith in me has been your salvation."

Finally, Jesus sends people away. "Go," he told the woman. But more. "Go in peace." The woman is to take God's love with her. She is to shine with his love, show forth to everyone in her life his forgiveness that is the heart of peace. Her joy will show everyone in her life the power of forgiveness that is the source of peace.

As an ordained minister, I can only ask, with deep regret and hope for radical change in the Christian churches, "Why do we not minister as Jesus ministers?"

Why do we not strive more consciously, publicly and conscientiously for holiness? Why do we put budgets and long-range planning on the front burner and holiness on the back burner? Why do we hesitate to speak of holiness as a viable option for ministers and for the people in the pew?

Why do we not point to sin as sin? Why are we so afraid to offend people?

In the Catholic Church, we have the Sacrament of Reconciliation. The sinner confesses and the priest expresses God's love and the community's joy in reconciliation as he pronounces forgiveness, in the name of God and Church, over the penitent. How sad, how terribly sad, that Catholics are so seldom encouraged to return to this magnificent sacrament. How very sad, too, that so many other Christian churches are bogged down in literalism and confusion and do not recognize the sacraments as the enfleshment of Jesus in human life, as the celebration and the effecting of God's forgiving, healing and transforming love in the lives of his people.

The Lord forgives. I think Christians need to spend time looking at a crucifix, not the namby-pamby kind with the risen Jesus reigning all pasty-faced on an ornate, sanded and varnished piece of mahogany. Look at a real crucifix that gives at least a hint of the price of redemption, the agony of the scourging, thorns and nails.

At St. Mary Magdalen's we have a huge crucifix in the sanctuary. The nails in the wrists and feet show the strain put on the flesh of Jesus. I have spent many hours gazing on that life-sized cross. I look at the nails in his hands and feet. At times, the Lord gives me a small insight into his suffering, into his pain-racked humanity as he redeems me.

It is not a pleasant insight, but one which fills me with gratitude for my salvation, for the Lord who died in my place.

Consider the Good Friday story, how Jesus was chosen to die and Barabbas was set free. One day, after reading a commentary on this Gospel story in *God's Word Today*, an excellent monthly magazine, I understood for the first time the meaning of Jesus' dying for me.

Picture Barabbas, if you will (see Matt. 27:15-26), waiting to be led out of his prison cell to be crucified. He apparently was going to be executed that day. He hears the crowd in the distance shouting, "Crucify him!" How frightened he must have been, believing the angry crowd was calling for his blood.

Then he hears the guards coming. He believes they are coming for him. He fears the nails, the whips, the shame of a naked, painful death before a jeering crowd. He cowers against the wall and the cell door flies open. There the guards stand. How terrified he must have been.

And then, a miracle! He hears, "You're free. Someone else is dying in your place."

What relief, what joy!

Each of us is like Barabbas. Because of sin we were destined to be separated from God for all eternity, to be separated from life, to experience a living death without end.

But Jesus died in our place. In his own humanity, he bridged the gap created by Adam. His humanity said, "Yes" where Adam's had said "No."

Reflecting on Barabbas has helped me understand what it means to have Jesus as my personal Savior. He has saved me from eternal death, a death I earned by my personal sins, a death I inherited through our sinful human nature.

The Church must also address the problem of social sin. Father James T. Burtchaell, in a book from the early 1970s, *Philemon's*

Problem, speaks of "engrained evil" in society. That means that evil exists systematically, in the core and heart of human institutions and relationships. It means that evil has become acceptable or at best it is ignored.

I remember an old Cajun woman who, when hearing about men cheating on their wives, would remark: "Well what do you expect? He's a man."

Engrained evil.

To accept evil as unavoidable, as natural, and to excuse it and even embrace it with some sort of good humor—that's engrained evil, and it is rooted in the basic sinfulness of individual human beings.

When Christians point out sin, they must be willing to look both into their own hearts and into their institutions, their government, the domestic and foreign budgets.

Look at America. Beautiful and wonderful America! God sheds his grace on you, America! But you need to repent. You claim you are the refuge of the world's hungry, poor and oppressed, but you set quotas and qualifications for immigration.

You kill innocent babies by the millions and you refuse aid to the poor while you stockpile grain and weapons.

You boast of freedom of religion, America, but you discourage belief in God by making sin attractive in business and entertainment. You like to talk about being "under God," but you deny God access to your courts, to public policy.

Indeed, there is such a thing as social sin—and we don't have to go to Russia, Latin America or Europe to find it.

Can you imagine what would happen in the world if the Christians in the U.S. would, like the prostitute in Luke, accept forgiveness and the commission to "Go in peace"? What if they actually began to forgive one another in their homes and churches, in their offices and fields? What if Christians went into the world of business, education and politics with the peace of God in their hearts and the blessing of peace on their lips?

Maybe we can't change the world. Maybe only a handful of Christians will forgive and be forgiven. But those who do will find God in their Middle.

Forgiveness is not theoretical. Forgiveness happens in the concrete of daily life—or it does not happen at all. Jesus said, in teaching us the Our Father and in the Sermon on the Mount, that if we do not forgive we cannot be forgiven.

Forgiveness is real, has flesh, and it hurts.

In the next chapter, I will deal with marriage. It, too, is an untapped power in the Christian mission. It, too, is a concrete place in which forgiveness must happen. If husbands and wives cannot forgive, they cannot be for the world what the Lord intends—lights of hope and peace, and a transforming and prophetic power.

Chapter 4

MAKING MARRIAGE CLICK

The man stopped me after a weekday Mass. His marriage was falling apart. He wanted to save it. In two weeks time, he had "found the Lord" and "completely changed" his life and his way of relating to his wife and children. He saw himself as a changed man—but his wife still wanted him out of the house.

What makes marriages fail? Why do so many people, who really want their marriages to succeed, end up in divorce or at best in unhealthy or strained relationships and unhappy homes?

I've heard a few quick responses to those questions, but somehow they fall flat and sound rather trite. One such answer is, "Well, they never had a Christian marriage in the first place!" Another, "If only they had taken time out to pray about their situation."

I firmly believe that some weddings performed in our Christian churches are not Christian marriages—and I can make that judgment, as you can, without being judgmental.

It is a fact that some people want a church wedding because "it is the thing to do" or "it'll give me something to look back on" or, believe it or not, "wedding pictures are prettier if they're taken in church."

I have talked to several young couples who wanted to get married in one church or another. I've asked them why they wanted a church wedding and they gave answers similar to those above.

Then I've asked them if they've prayed about their marriage, if

49

they've sought counsel, if they've talked about faith, religion, family size, whether both will work or only one will work. Usually, they answered, "Oh, we talked some."

In each case, I suggested to the young couples that they not bother the Church with their wedding since they were not planning a Christian marriage but a secular one. I've suggested to each one that they go to a justice of the peace or merely hop over a broom as was the custom in certain secions of frontier America.

Needless to say, they didn't take my suggestion to heart. I think the ministers who married these young couples in their churches prostituted their ministry and their churches.

I know that ministers feel caught in the middle when people, who are not ready for marriage, ask them to perform the ceremony. But there is no excuse other than ignorance, greed or cowardice for a Christian minister to officiate in his church at a mock Christian marriage.

I see two major social factors contributing to the instability of marriage. One is the fact that divorce is so acceptable, even among Christians. The second is the breakdown of traditional sexual morals and the traditional role models of men and women.

Divorce is so acceptable in society because certain Christian churches have forsaken their responsibility and become mere wedding mills. Somehow these churches are no longer custodians of the Word of God that sets Christian marriage up as a holy covenant, a covenant that gives flesh to God's covenant with his people.

I will talk about how the churches can help us cope with these factors. Then I will talk about what people must do, when they are caught in the middle of a troublesome relationship, to work out their problems, if they can be worked out at all.

First, the churches.

Some divorces cannot be avoided. Some people will marry even when the Church tells them their marriages are doomed to failure. Some marriages, even when everything has been done properly, will fail. People change. People become influenced by selfishness, greed, lust or what have you and relationships are strained to the breaking point.

But Christians themselves accept divorce as a viable alternative to a difficult marriage. I believe this openness to divorce makes a farce of the wedding vows, "for better or worse, for richer or poorer, in sickness and in health, till death do us part." Christian ministers should not let people proclaim those vows in their churches unless they are sure the people are committed to a permanent marriage.

Some ministers who fail to prepare couples for permanent relationships are quick to put the burden on God for reconciling spouses: "Let us ask the Lord to give us a miracle, let us ask him to miraculously heal this marriage."

There are no "miraculous answers" for people who are in difficult marriages. Granted, God can and does work miracles, but he doesn't violate free will. If a man is domineering, faithless and unfaithful, it is doubtful that he will change instantaneously into a model of virtue. God may bombard him with grace and he may have a bona-fide conversion experience, but conversion is only the starting point. The man has to change, to grow, and this does not happen miraculously most of the time.

People can and must work their way through difficulties and reconciliation.

I know of one or two cases where people have really changed dramatically almost overnight. I know of many more cases in which people claimed instant healing and conversion and such was not the case. They had merely brainwashed themselves into believing they were changed, hoping their enthusiasm would convince their alienated husbands and wives of their new-found goodness and thus head off separation and divorce.

Couples must prepare well for marriage.

In many Catholic dioceses in the U.S. people seeking a church wedding are required to go through a lengthy period of prayer, study, reflection, psychological testing and counseling. There are very few teen-age marriages performed in the Church, and when a pregnancy is involved, the Church is doubly cautious in letting people enter into marriage.

Personal spiritual growth, before and after marriage, is a growing emphasis in the Catholic Church. There are good processes and programs offered, such as Marriage Encounter, Cursillo, Engaged Encounter, Charismatic Renewal, RENEW and so on.

I am convinced, however, that the most effective education happens in the local church and through its pulpit and formation programs. Without spiritual direction and nourishment in the local church, without conversion and reconversion, without growth and challenge, people fall victim to undesirable social values and pressures.

Churches must develop good counseling programs to help people who are in serious marital difficulties. But, first things first, churches will have to start preaching the Gospel as though it can be lived, as though it is relevant, as though Jesus is Lord and Master, as though faith in him gives us power to overcome sin and to change things.

Broken people must be healed. Broken, unhealed people will not have much chance at success in second, third or fourth marriages.

Christian churches must help people discover themselves and their God, accept Jesus as Lord and Savior and center their lives in a Christian community before they can hope to succeed in the adventure of Christian marriage.

For Catholics, a Christian marriage is called a "sacramental marriage." The word "sacrament" comes from the Latin meaning a "sign" or special mark that was placed on soldiers so everyone would know they were in the service of the emperor.

So, for the Catholic, the Sacrament of Baptism "signs" them for the Lord. And it does more. In the ritual of the sacrament, Catholics believe that God does what he promises to do—forgives sin, fills with grace and lives within the Christian.

Marriage, as a sacrament, becomes for Catholics an experience of God dwelling intimately with the married couple. Admittedly, all too few Catholics understand and live that reality. But nevertheless, it is true.

Admittedly, any Christian marriage is sacramental and has God dwelling intimately in the union of husband and wife. Unfortunately, theologies other than the Catholic one make it almost impossible to express this reality.

So, I turn to the highest Catholic authority to explain the power and holiness of sacramental marriage, the pope.

Pope John Paul II, in 1981, wrote a magnificent document on Christian marriage and family life. With the ominous title of "Apostolic Exhortation on Family," the document offers a prophetic vision of Christian marriage.

After reading John Paul's document, I am convinced that sacramental, conjugal love is the most underestimated Christian power in the Church today, a power that literally could change the face of the earth if unleashed by good catechesis, support of faith communities, evangelical preaching and a better theology of marriage.

As a Catholic I find it necessary to emphasize "conjugal" in speaking of marital love. Because of an exaggerated appreciation of celibacy, most Catholics have not sufficiently understood Holy Matrimony and the power of conjugal love.

Pope John Paul II formalizes through his teaching the reality many Christian couples have experienced, if not vocalized, in their conjugality.

John Paul says that in our conjugality, we who are married sacramentally "memorialize all of salvation history."

He says that, in our conjugality, we "actuate what happened on the Cross."

And he says that, in our conjugality, we "prophesy the second coming of Christ."

What does this mean? Can the Holy Father be serious that conjugal lovers, in their conjugality, in their beds, in their sexual union actually synopsize the mystery of salvation, that they make present the redeeming sacrifice and love of the Crucified Lord, that they, in their conjugal embrace, proclaim that Jesus Christ will come again?

Can he really mean this?

He means it. But he gives "conjugality" a broader scope than do most people.

Look at the meaning of sacramental conjugality through the eyes of St. Paul in Ephesians 5:21 and following. St. Paul teaches that the union of husband and wife is like the union of Jesus and his Church. This means that married couples can learn what marriage means by looking at the relationship of Jesus and his Church.

And that is what St. Paul does.

After telling husbands and wives to submit to one another in Christ, to love one another mutually, and to die to self for the sake of the other, the Apostle outlines what this means.

St. Paul sees a covenant relationship between Jesus and his Church. He sees enfleshed in this relationship the promise of Yahweh that "I will be your God and you will be my people."

Here, in the Church, God becomes more intimate. God becomes husband in the person of Jesus, laying down his life so that his bride, the Church, may be made holy. This, Paul says, is what husbands must do. They must die to self in their love for their wives. Their wives' relationships with God is the most important consideration for husbands. Since the wife and husband are in the image of Church and Christ, the man, in Paul's mind, represents Christ to the wife; but, if we read Paul carefully, we know that the wife represents Christ to the husband because she is Church to him and Church is nothing less than the incarnated Christ continuing in the world his work of salvation.

St. Paul teaches that the husband's loving sacrifice purifies and sanctifies the wife (and therefore himself since he is one with her). The husband is, to Paul, more obviously Jesus and priest in the union, but since both are one flesh and one spirit, they share co-equally in the mystery of covenanted love.

It is impossible for Jesus to be more in the husband or more in the wife within the sacrament. The sacrament is "both-being-one" in Christ. If they are one, there can be no distinction of greater or lesser, of primary or secondary, of more power and less power. The destruction of marriages begins in this fight for dominance, for primacy. The fight may be subtle, even subconscious, but it is real. The husband and wife fall victim to the notion that submissiveness is subservience, that one or the other, usually the woman, has to prove he or she is as good or better than the other.

This is not a Christian notion of marriage. For the Christian couple, there can be no competition, no put-down, no subservience. Joe is not Joe without Mary. Mary is not Mary without Joe. Joe and Mary are who they are because they are Joe and Mary, each loving the other without reservation or condition. They love unconditionally. That is submissiveness, not subservience.

Because they love unconditionally, the Christian couple does "memorialize all of salvation history." God's covenant takes flesh in their fidelity, their constant willingness to forgive, to make room for weakness, to offer strength and support.

Theirs is a covenanted love, a mutual dying for the sake of the beloved. They are together and mutually offering themselves as sacrifice for the other. That is a mutual, redemptive, priestly act.

They mutually give life, which is a creative act, a loving act. They give physical life to their children—and they give spiritual life to one another in their conjugal, sacramental spirituality. And they help one another toward holiness, a sanctifying ministry.

To look into the life of a sacramental couple is to look at a microcosm of Church, of salvation history. The couple's moods and movements, their risings and fallings, their successes and their failures, their holiness and their sinfulness reflect, echo, magnify, particularize and proclaim the rising, falling and rising again of the People of God. The life of the community of husband and wife captures in such a personal and intimate way the life of God and his entire people.

When husband and wife bring children into the world and sustain this new life through their charity, they give witness to the creativity and providence of God.

When husband and wife forgive, people are reminded of God's promise to forgive. When people see mere humans loving themselves and their God in good times and in bad, they are more prone to believe in a God who loves in good times and in bad.

How can anyone, serious about Christianity, fail to capture, savor and preach this magnificent truth?

And more.

John Paul II says that in our sacramental conjugality we "actualize" what happened on the Cross.

That boggles the mind! We, in our huffing and puffing of passionate conjugality, make the redeeming love of Jesus present? Is this not almost blasphemous?

Not at all.

We need to understand the term "conjugality." It is like "sexuality." Too many people, when it comes to these terms, focus only on sex organs and orgasms. Sexuality involves what it means to be totally man, totally woman. Conjugality involves what it means to be totally husband, totally wife.

To love conjugally is to be conjugal when separated by many miles. It is to be conjugal where separated during a workday, or to be together at the supermarket or kitchen cabinet.

In other words, whatever conjugal lovers do, within the context of sacramental love, they do conjugally. They cannot, for even a moment, cease to be conjugal lovers. Conjugality is as much alive at Mass on Sunday as it is in bed or in the birthing room of the local hospital.

So, yes indeed, sacramental conjugal lovers do make present the redemptive love of Jesus—but not simply because they "have sex" or because they "remain faithful" or because they do not practice artificial birth control.

All these have bearing on making the reality of the Cross present in life—but most of all, sacramental lovers make Jesus present because of two things: (1) the sacrament, and (2) the love.

1. A sacrament (according to the old *Baltimore Catechism*) is an outward sign of inward grace. That can mean only one thing— the real presence of Jesus. If matrimony is a sacrament, it is the real presence of Jesus. In the union of wife and husband, Jesus is really present just as surely as he is present in the Eucharist. He is present perhaps in a different way. Man and woman remain man and woman completely while bread and wine no longer remain bread and wine. But if marriage is a sacrament, it is an outward sign of inward grace, it is Jesus.

If the sacrament is the real presence of Jesus, then marriage does make present what happened on the Cross—it makes present the redeeming and loving and saving action of Christ. Sacramental conjugality makes salvation present!

What an awesome reality! What a challenging truth! What a call to holiness, to fidelity, to chastity, to a life of prayerful and loving self-giving!

2. And then there is love.

Of course, it is hard to distinguish love from the sacrament, because "God is love and he who loves abides in God and God in him." Where God abides, there is the redeeming love of Jesus, the mystery of the Cross.

But let's speak of love as the sacrificing action of wife for husband and husband for wife. It is in this sense that love is separate from sacrament. There is an ebb and flow to the expression and experience of love. It is constant but not static. Love becomes, it remains, it grows and manifests itself through the dynamics of living for the other.

The love Peg has for me is a redemptive love. During my drinking days, when we were both caught in the middle of alcoholism, she probably never thought of her love as a redeeming force. Now there is no doubt in either of our minds that her love, her suffering because of my affliction, somehow became one with the suffering of Jesus and was offered with Jesus on the Cross for me.

Her sacrificial, conjugal love made the Cross present in our marriage, to those who really knew the depth of the problem.

Some men and women would think a wife or husband crazy for putting up with that kind of misery. Maybe we who love in that way are a little crazy, for it is a life of constant forgiving, of constant giving up of one's rights. It is really being a fool for Jesus.

But the dynamics of love are not always so demanding and painful. The redeeming love of Jesus is made present when a husband surprises his wife, in love, with a new ring, or a single flower, or a new car, or an evening out. The redeeming love of Jesus is present when a wife sews a button on her husband's shirt, or cooks a meal, or irons a shirt, or goes to the office, or visits the sick or cares for him when he is sick.

As Mother Angelica so often says, "Because you are married, when you do the dishes, the Trinity does the dishes!"

Now that's a mouthful, is it not? But it's true. God is the primary community. When we are holy, we enter into God as God enters into us. We enter that union of Father, Son, Spirit. We become benefactors of that grace, temples of that God. He lives in us, moves with us, gives life and meaning to all our actions.

That's why there is such dignity and power in matrimony. It is a state in life just like Holy Orders.

That is why sin is so terrible a thing in marriage. To abuse human sexuality, to forsake vows, to be unfaithful, to ignore the powerful presence of the Lord in such a day-to-day, seemingly humdrum life experience is to tell God to move over or to move out, that your agenda is more important than his.

Finally, Pope John Paul II says that conjugal lovers prophesy the second coming of Christ.

I think this is explained very simply. The kind of love it takes to love sacramentally makes no sense if we don't believe Jesus is Lord and that he meant what he said, that he is coming again, that his Kingdom will be fulfilled and that we expect to be part of that Kingdom.

The Kingdom, however, must have meaning now or it is not the

Lord's Kingdom. He said the Kingdom was within us. We must have joy now. We must experience healing and freedom now or his Kingdom is a lie. We must experience deliverance now. Jesus saw Satan falling from heaven before creation. He saw this again when his disciples began to heal and cast out demons.

The pope speaks the truth. Truth will set you free, even if you can't yourself explain that truth. Truth is not words, it is relationship; truth is not doctrine for doctrine only formulates truth. Truth is what is, not what should be. God is. Jesus himself said, "I am the way, the truth, the life."

To know truth is to know Jesus. That is relationship. Once relationship is present, then loving hearts must speak words that try so feebly to express what the heart already knows. Look at couples in love. How long does it take them to say and mean, "I love you." In courtship, "I love you" means that "Among all others, you are my special one, my only one."

After years of marital fidelity and mutual sacrifice, "I love you" means "There is no other. I know you, I am you, I can no longer know me apart from you."

Churches must begin again to preach sexual morality, but not as a law imposed from above. Sexual morality must become a sign of love that springs from the heart that has experienced grateful repentance, conversion and now is ready for servant love.

Now, let's look at people and relationships.

As director of young-adult ministry in our parish, I see young men and women who long for intimacy, for a special someone. Many find true love. Others are still looking, shopping really, with a blueprint in mind of the perfect man or woman—and Mr. Perfect or Miss Perfect is always someone who will complement "me," whose love for "me" will make "me" happy and hopefully Mr. or Miss Perfect will be happy, too, as he or she makes "me" happy.

In America especially, people live according to the Gospel of Instant Gratification. Many people consider themselves too precious and important to have to wait for any pleasure, any reward. They are as the center of their universe and God (certain preachers contribute to this terrible blasphemy!) is a puppet on a string waiting to dance at their command. If only they use the right scripture or words, he *must* grant our every prayer. What hogwash!

I have found that even among serious young Christians there is a lot of contamination by this self-centered, convenient Christianity, to say nothing of modern secular influence.

There is a lot of sexual contact going on before marriage. And yet, this abuse of sex has its roots in something most human, most beautiful.

The use of sex, even in this unhealthy and sinful way, is the result of a craving for love, a craving for intimacy, a craving for the perfect union. These young adults are really caught in the middle. They want fulfillment, need fulfillment but are unequipped or unable to find that fulfillment within traditional norms of moral behavior. They mistake the superficial for the real thing—or worse, they compromise their principles and establish the superficial as the ultimate in relationship. This frees them from sharing what real love demands—life, brokenness, gifts, growth.

Sex outside of marriage (premarital, extramarital or homosexual) is a lie.

Sexual intimacy speaks of total dedication, of exclusive love, of the creative, life-giving power of God. In sexual intercourse, a man and woman in love reveal themselves totally. Nakedness says, "I give myself totally to you." Sexual intercourse, the language of love, says, "I give you myself without reservation, exclusively, forever." If there is love without reservation, there is openness to life. How can one be completely without reservation and open to life in premarital (uncommitted), adulterous (idolatrous, selfish) and homosexual (forbidden and unnatural) sexual experiences and relationships?

Sure, people will say, "Oh, that is only how you see it."

That is how God sees it.

It's clear through the traditional teaching of all mainline and evangelical Christian churches that sexual intercourse is reserved for marriage. Aside from the dangers to society that arise through sexual promiscuity—the breakdown of family, the loss of respect for fellow human beings, the emphasis on personal pleasure and gratification regardless of the feelings and needs of others—the damage of promiscuity to individuals is reason enough for people to cherish chastity.

Promiscuity kills intimacy. Referring to a newspaper article in which it was reported a woman had been "intimate" with many men, a close friend exclaimed, "Intimate! She went public!"

Sexual activity is not automatically synonymous with "intimacy" or with "love."

Intimacy can exist without sexual contact. Intimacy is a union of spirit, of soul, of heart. Sexual intercourse is one way, a beautiful way, of expressing intimacy, but of itself, it does not create intimacy. Intimacy is born of love, not sex.

A person cannot love through sex if love does not exist in the first place. You can't "make love"! Love without sex is still love; sex without love is a lie.

Abuse of sex, sleeping around, promiscuity—you name it—destroys the language of conjugal love. If a person has used sex indiscriminately, selfishly, promiscuously, how can that person's sexuality, his or her "language of love," speak of total commitment and mean it? How can abused sexuality say, "I love you and you alone. Through my nakedness, my language of undefiled and total commitment, I give myself to you and you alone"? That "language" has been used time and again in nonintimate sex. The language has been abused and its power to communicate meaning has been weakened if not destroyed.

So sexual activity outside marriage is dangerous to individuals and to future marriages. Sociologists say that people who are sexually active before marriage are more likely to commit adultery after they are married than those who remain chaste before marriage. Once the language of love has been abused, it is difficult to make it mean something. Abused human sexuality to some degree loses its power to communicate what it was intended to communicate—both love and life.

However, thanks be to God, forgiveness, repentance, reformation can restore to a person the spiritual power of sex to communicate love. That is the marvelous thing about God's redeeming love, about the power of the Sacrament of Reconciliation. Broken, sorrowful and needy people can come before their God and Church and be assured of forgiveness, full acceptance by the community and full restoration of all spiritual power to do good.

I know firsthand the burning passion of sexual attraction. I, as much as anyone else, can be affected by the allurements of modern cinema, literature and television. Sex is everywhere, in all sorts of perversions, and is acceptable, perversions and all.

It is perhaps the most obvious personal and social problem today. In a later chapter, I will treat temptation and how people can face temptation more calmly and successfully.

For the moment, let's just say that the Lord is victorious and his disciples are victorious with him if they rely on his Word, his power, his love.

I am not speaking here of an exaggerated literalist approach to scripture and faith. I am talking about Catholic spirituality, about living the power of the Spirit.

If this book about people caught in the middle has any goal at all, it is to tell people they can be set free from sin, from self-hatred, from oppression, from bondage. In the next chapter, I will discuss how we can personally enter into the powerful life of the Spirit.

As a final word to the churches concerning their responsibility, and especially to the Catholic Church, I want to ask whether the Church could accept two kinds of valid, licit marriages while preserving the notion of a marriage that speaks of covenant. This could help make what we now call "sacramental marriage" more meaningful and effective as a missionary force in the Church.

In so doing, I know I am putting myself in The Middle where some people are concerned. Some will say this smacks of bad theology, of a departure from what the magisterium holds regarding Holy Matrimony. For me, what I am about to suggest makes sense. But I realize that my ideas do not automatically make sound doctrine or acceptable discipline simply because they make sense to me and appeal to me and others.

I am most certainly not teaching what the Church is not teaching. I am asking questions, making propositions, urging the magisterium to reexamine marriage, to come up with a better way of defining sacramental matrimony in the light of higher rather than lower standards, to reverse the deterioration of marriage and family life. If competent Church authority finds my questions divisive and/or beyond the scope of present pastoral consideration, I withdraw them. It is that simple. I am a son of the Church.

We all know that not all marriages work. Consummation alone does not a marriage make. If sexual intercourse were all that went into a marriage, many supposedly single people would suddenly find themselves married—perhaps to many others.

We know, too, because of our own annulment processes, that a sacramental marriage is not guaranteed simply because a man and woman exchange vows before a priest and then have sexual intercourse.

The Catholic Church, in many cases, is granting annulments, saying that in spite of following proper procedure and rituals (such as marriage before a priest of two baptized Catholics), no sacramental marriage truly existed.

An annulment is not a "Catholic divorce." An annulment states only that a sacramental marriage never existed in spite of everyone's understanding and good intentions at the time.

In other cases, the Church is not granting annulments because the Church believes a sacramental marriage does indeed take place.

I have no problem with this.

The Church has this authority.

More is required to constitute a sacramental marriage, it seems to me, than meeting a few external criteria established by canon law. There must be a faith dimension to sacramental marriage or sacramental marriage just doesn't make sense.

Here are a couple of admittedly difficult questions.

1. Can the Church begin to broaden its understanding of approved and acceptable marriages to allow for marriages, other than sacramental, within the communion of the Church? Can the Church, for example, officially recognize civil marriages as valid, though not sacramental, and permit Catholics in those marriages to receive the Eucharist?

I realize I am on dangerous ground here. But the Church does place great credence in "consummation" of the marriage, in other words in sealing the vows with sexual intercourse.

My point is this: If a couple really loves each other, marries civilly and seals their vows with sexual intercourse, are they not truly married? For nealy twelve centuries, the Catholic Church did not have as much to say about marriage as it does today. Were all those marriages in the past non-Christian, nonsacramental? If not, why not? If civil marriages then were approved by the Church without penalty to the couples themselves, why not today?

But, the objection is raised, if such civil marriages were today recognized as Christian and couples were allowed to receive Communion, what would be the point of having some couples marry with the full blessing of the Church?

The advantage would be this—sacramental marriages would be recognized only among couples who had reached a level of spiritual commitment that made their marriage a sign of covenant, a sign of God-with-us. These would truly be sacramental marriages.

And if this idea is preposterous and unacceptable, I do have "Plan B." It follows.

2. Could the Church state that all marriages between Catholics, who are committed to a permanent marriage, are sacramental, once consummated, whether they are performed civilly or in a church? Actually, the Church now recognizes marriages other than Catholic as sacramental. If such were ever possible, a new designation of meaning and honor would be made for marriages involving couples who had reached a level of maturity and spiritual commitment that made their marriage a sign of covenant, a sign of God-with-us.

I was totally surprised during the writing of this section of *Caught in the Middle* to learn that these ideas are far from new. Several theologians around the world have had such thoughts. And in France, the Church as been experimenting with such an approach to marriage.

In an article in *Studia Canonica*, Dr. James A. Schmeiser, of Kings College, London, Ontario, writes that in the French experiment there are three recognized forms of marriage. In the Diocese of Autun, couples considering marriage are informed of the three forms of marriage recognized by the Church: civil marriage, welcomed civil marriage and sacramental marriage.

According to Dr. Schmeiser, civil marriage "takes place at city hall and is registered with the State. The Church recognizes the value of the human commitment of this marriage, and even if the State permits divorce, the Church recognizes the possibility of a permanent commitment." The Church is prepared to "welcome" such couples if they are prepared to affirm a faith dimension in their lives.

The scholar writes that welcomed civil marriages are for couples who are Christian by baptism but who are distant from the Church. They are not interested in celebrating their marriage sacramentally because "sacrament" has little meaning for them. They believe in God, however, and want to express their new relationship in terms of their own level of faith. The Church, "in an attitude of love and hospitality," wants to remain open to such couples, to give them a sign of faith through its own ministry and the presence of its committed Christian couples. A celebration takes place in a church or in a home, involves "a ritual of welcome, readings (scriptural or secular), declaration of intentions, exchange of rings, and a prayer which summarizes the intention of the couple in specific areas. It is clearly understood that this is not the sacrament of marriage. The marriage is registered in a special ecclesial register."

Finally, the Diocese of Autun celebrates sacramental matrimony for "those who have deepened their Christian faith and who wish to symbolize the covenant of Christ and his people in their relationship" in the way I have described marriage above.

Needless to say, one wonders just how long the Vatican will allow this "experiment" to continue. Autun's "levels of marriage" seem to make tremendous sense, especially if one is familiar with the work done by several important psychologists on levels of spiritual and moral maturity—such as Kohlberg and Fisher. We can only hope and pray that responsible authorities in the Church are willing to be open to new ideas, and that the innovators in the Church are willing to listen to authority in the Church.

It seems to me that we, the Church, could save ourselves a lot of time, trouble and misunderstanding if we could make some sort of adjustment in our Church marriage laws. I'm not speaking about denying truth or doing away with the sacredness of marriage, but of trying to find a better way of expressing the Church's teaching and seeing it achieved in daily life. It seems to me we have cheapened the entire concept of sacramental marriage by placing physical consummation and canonical form above the most fundamental elements in Christian life and in a Christian marriage, namely, love and faith.

Without love, can a sacramental marriage exist? Can an unloving union mirror the relationship between Christ and Church, memorialize all of salvation history, actuate what happens on the Cross and prophesy the second coming of Jesus?

Without faith, there is no Christian. Without at least one Christian, can there be a Christian marriage? The new Code of Canon Law no longer claims as Catholics those who have formally left the Church to join another denomination. Is it a far step to demand personal faith in Jesus Christ as a fundamental ingredient in what it means to be Christian and to enter in Christian marriage or into any sacramental experience? Doesn't the absence of personal faith, in an adult baptized person, call into question that person's membership in the Church? Is membership in the Church determined solely by God's gift of faith in baptism—or does not the person's reciprocal faith in God have just as much to do with his or her Christian identity and membership in the Church?

Personal faith—here is the key to most of the Catholic Church's gravest problems. People follow ritual. They believe, to be sure, there is a God, but Catholics by and large do not place great emphasis on a dynamic, personal relationship with Jesus Christ. I can't speak for other mainline churches, but I'm afraid they experience the same problem.

It seems, at times, that some baptized persons try to believe vicariously—through the "faith of the Church." They sort of plug into worship and sacraments. In this way they hope they are plugged into heaven and are safe from hell. Somehow they see no need personally to look into the gentle eyes of their Savior.

Theirs is the camouflaged Jesus, the Jesus of beautiful vestments, the Jesus of Sunday Mass and Good Friday dirges, the Jesus of great music and of good feelings at Christmas and Easter. Theirs is the Jesus who hides in a wafer but never speaks directly to people in their bedrooms, offices or automobiles. Theirs is a Jesus somehow communicated through ritual, through ministry, through priest, bishop and pope, but never through the embrace of sacramental lovers, never in the advice of a Christian friend.

Their Jesus is imprisoned, kept small and precious, in tabernacles of gold, in the cool fleshless embrace of intellectual acknowledgment. This Jesus is never allowed to roam freely in the fullness of the Spirit, in their spirits, to touch, to convict, to forgive, to heal, to inspire, to challenge, to caress, to admonish, to cleanse. Because these baptized persons have created God in their own image, because they have kept God too small, they are idolators.

A God created in our own image is only a hero-God. A hero is admired because he incorporates the worshiper's values. He is not loved for himself. The hero is not an innovator, a creator. He is, in essence, a follower. He has the vision of his "worshipers" or he is not their hero. He is a rescuer, but not a savior. He can save people only from those they believe are their enemies, but he can never save them from themselves. They expect him to listen to them. They do not listen to him.

Jesus is not a hero. His is the vision of the Father; his are the values of the Father, not ours.

I am sure there are millions of Christians of all denominations who have created God in their own image. Perhaps we all do this to some degree. God is indeed too big to hold, too deep to fathom. We can get only so much of him into our minds, our hearts.

That's why the saints have stopped trying to get God into themselves. They seek, rather, to lose themselves in God. And that is what prayer is all about. I want to go into prayer later. For now, let's consider what it takes to make a marriage a Christian marriage, what it takes to renew tired marriages.

I have seen some Catholic and other Christian couples who, in spite of their best efforts, cannot make their marriages ring with joy, cannot achieve more than tolerance in their relationships. These are people who go to Church, work in the Church, support the Church. But they are people who are not filled with joy. They feel the weight of failure in love, of incompatibility, of hopelessness. They find no meaning in life. It is as though love ended with the honeymoon, as though Prince Charming and Princess Pretty have lost their ability to love. Yet, they want their marriages to succeed. They want to love. They try and try to capture or recapture that missing thing which gives thrills, a link with all of life, a handle on their own self-worth.

I wish I could tell them simply to "pray and God will take care of everything," but I cannot. While I believe with all my heart and soul that God does heal and does work miracles, Christian relationships are built on faith—personal faith in a personal God, a personal Savior who founded a Church and calls us to a personal relationship with him in that Church.

As I've implied earlier, it is not "faithful" to ask God to wave his holy hand over you and change you against your will. God is not like that. He gave you a free will. He will not take that back. He wants your love—but love is an act of the will, not an emotion, not an orgasm, not a contract, not a conditional relationship. Love is the will saying, "All for you. What is best for you is what I want."

When people are so desperately seeking "happiness" and a "meaningful" relationship, they so often are looking for things to come *their* way. God says that is not real love. Real love is to die to self for the good of the other. So your husband is a bore; he is no longer the romantic rogue that brought you to the marital chamber; he snores and burps and makes other unpleasant and unromantic noises. If you love him, you embrace him as he is, serve him as he is.

The same is true for husbands who feel their wives have lost their glamor, sex appeal, sense of humor, energy and freshness. Love leads a man to see beyond the superficial, to see the spirit of his spouse, to see that soul which yearns for the Lord as a doe yearns for running streams. The Christian husband will love such a wife into life. He will see her despondency, her impatience, her unhappiness as an opportunity to serve her, to comfort her, to challenge her, to lead her into the embrace of the Lord who alone can satisfy her longing. And the Lord's embrace will be felt in the husband's arms, not in a myriad of church or social activities, chairmanships and charity balls.

It is not easy to move from selfish pursuit of happiness to selfless service in joy.

This comes only through spiritual growth, through dying and rising, through successes that build on failures. Such a transformation comes not from one's own powers to change himself or herself, but from trusting submission to the Lord, to seeking his healing within the suffering of dying and rising, to seek blessing from his crucified hand, to seek wisdom from his Spirit, to seek life from his Father.

But is this not a contradiction? A moment ago I said that we could not depend on God to work miracles to heal us, that we had to use our free will. No, it is not a contradiction. The secret, if there is a secret, lies in this. The first thing we seek with our free will is total submission to the Lord. This is the act of love upon which all other expressions of love depend.

The person who seeks cheap miracles merely asks God for favors and gives God nothing in return. The person who really seeks healing and transformation seeks first of all to love God and to please him with a total gift of self. It is from that relationship that personal healing grows. From personal healing grow healings of relationships.

It is not easy to admit we are powerless to change ourselves. But this is true. The greatest lie of the medical profession today deals with self-healing, with the ability of thinking or wishing ourselves into wholeness, into health, into happiness and self-respect.

Modern psychology lies. It says that there is healing power in positive thinking. This attitude makes oneself one's savior. It makes sin and grace meaningless. All power lies in the person's mind, and if you are not healing yourself it is because you have a bad self-image and you can heal that yourself.

Hogwash!

Only the Lord is Savior and healer. True, we must go to him, we must help ourselves, but we do not heal ourselves. He does.

There are people in hopeless marriages. For these people, divorce and annulment may be the only way out, the only hope for happiness and for joy, for a meaningful and productive life, for successful discipleship.

A decision that one's marriage is hopeless can come only after much prayer, reflection and consultation. Married people are part of the faith-community, of the secular community. What happens to them and what they do affects everyone. They do not live isolated lives. They are not responsible only for themselves. The second greatest lie that Satan has told in this last half of the twentieth century is that we are responsible only to and for ourselves, that what we do is no one else's business. The biggest lie of all, that so many people have believed, is that Satan himself does not exist and, therefore, neither do temptation, evil, sin. From there, it is only a short step to believing that God does not exist.

A decision that one's marriage is worth saving and can be saved also comes through consultation, prayer and reflection.

But I believe that personal conversion is necessary for both husband and wife if a Christian marriage is to be renewed, healed and strengthened.

Peg and I experienced a tremendous renewal of our marriage after Sister Briege prayed with me. But the renewal didn't come "miraculously out of the blue." No. I had to die to self. I had to admit I was an alcoholic. I had to suffer as Peg had suffered. I had to go through a terrible fire, a terrible humiliation, a desert, a crucifixion. Then came the resurrection—sobriety. Then came the glory —a deeper, happier and more joyful relationship with Peg and the beginning of a new life of love and ministry.

We began with cradle faith, a groping, growing faith, a desire for faith. I had always wanted to be holy as, I am sure, Peg desires holiness. But I was weak, broken, alternately denying my sin and trying to heal myself, believing I was beyond forgiveness but desperately wanting forgiveness, caught in the middle between despair and a nagging hope whose ultimate source could only be the Hound of Heaven.

In the last couple of years before I actually stopped drinking, I had prayed long and hard for sobriety—but I didn't want actually to stop drinking. I wanted God to wave his holy hand over me. I wanted him to make my decision for me, to take away the pain of decision, to shield me from seeing my own sickness and from having to admit I was, I am, an alcoholic.

Happily, God is wiser than we are. He made me do it the hard way. He made me see myself as I am. He made me make a choice, exercise my will. He made me depend on others—and in that great gift of shared love, I discovered a life-changing truth: I am indeed loveable.

Today, I am healed.

People from Alcoholics Anonymous don't like to hear me say that I am healed—and they have good reason. Alcoholism is a disease. One drink is one too many. While I claim I am healed, I still cannot take, do not want to take, that first drink.

In this I claim healing. Through prayer, I have lost all desire to drink. That is the healing. But for perhaps hundreds of thousands of other people, there may be no healing of the desire to drink. Many have to continue to go to A.A. meetings, to have counseling. God is answering their prayers for sobriety in a different way—but he is answering their prayers just as he answers mine. I, too, must pray for continued sobriety, depend on my Lord that the desire will not return, or that if it does return, I will have his strength and help to resist the desire.

But I am ahead of myself. I think, for the sake of those who know me but do not believe I am an alcoholic, and for the sake of all readers, I must tell the story of how God healed me of addiction to alcohol.

It was Friday, September 2, 1977. An empty bottle of Scotch whiskey lay on its side on the table. It had been half full when I began drinking it three hours before, as I listened to some religious tapes.

The Scotch had followed two six-packs of beer. I had killed one at home that Thursday evening and one at a friend's house. It was one of those evenings when I had to drink until I passed out.

I remember looking at my watch as I made my way to bed. It was 3:00 A.M. I passed out before I hit the pillow.

At 5:00 A.M. I came fully awake. I got out of bed and went into the kitchen. I felt shame, a deep burning shame. It had happened again. Time after time I would end up drunk.

Time after time I would tell myself that I could control it. I would beg God to "make me like everybody else" so I could have a couple of social drinks and be able to stop.

Two weeks before I had decided to go to Alcoholics Anonymous. A priest-friend was a recovering alcoholic and he had agreed to take me to my first meeting. I hadn't told Peg about my decision. I guess I wanted to leave myself an out—and I found one, one that I called a "family emergency" when I called Father John to explain why I couldn't go.

For weeks, as I prayed for healing, I could hear a distinct little voice say, over and over again, "Go to A.A." That's why I had decided to go in the first place, although I insisted to the Lord that I was not "one of those people," that he could heal me on his own if only he would.

So, at 5:00 A.M. on September 2, 1977, nearly a year after Briege had prayed with me and I had felt the searing love of the Lord, I sat in my kitchen, with a terrible hangover, nauseated, filled with shame and remorse.

I'm convinced there is no greater remorse than that of an alcoholic the morning after the night before—unless it would be the remorse of an unfaithful husband or wife.

So I sat there at the kitchen table, feeling dirty, less than a man, terrified that I was in over my head and could do nothing to control my drinking.

I prayed again, "Lord, make me like other people. Heal me Lord that I can have a couple of drinks like everybody else."

Again, the little, inner voice said, "Go to A.A."

I insisted that the Lord heal me on his own.

Again, "Go to A.A."

Finally, I said, "Lord, if this is really you talking to me, if you really want me to go to A.A., you'll have to give me a sign because I AM NOT one of THOSE people!"

A few moments later, Peg came into the kitchen and said something she had never said before, something she had never even hinted at. She put her hand on my shoulder and said, "Honey, do you want me to go to an A.A. meeting with you?"

I knew this was the Lord's sign. It was clear to me. She didn't know about the earlier decision to go to A.A. I had never mentioned A.A.

I looked up at her and said with a great sense of peace and determination, "No, that won't be necessary. I have to do this on my own."

And, by the grace of God, I did.

That following Sunday, I went to A.A. with Father John.

When I got home that night, I went to bed and was almost asleep when suddenly I sat up in bed, filled with the realization that I had been healed. I told Peg, "Honey, I'm healed."

Peg said, "Yes, I know."

And I knew it was true.

From that moment to now, I have never craved a drink. I miss cold beer. I like cold beer. But I no longer crave it. I do not have cold beer.

I'm a bit overweight because I compensate with sweets for the booze I can't have, but it came to me in Lent of 1986 that, although I do eat well, I fast every day, because every day I say "no" to a cold beer.

In the summer of 1977, about seven months after Sister Briege had prayed for me, I called her, admitted I had a "little drinking problem" and asked for her prayers.

She prayed with me over the phone and had one of her "visions" that, at the time, I wished she had kept to herself.

"Henry, I see you going down a long and narrow road and you are all alone. And in the road is a deep, deep pit. It is very deep and steep and you fall into the pit. You try and try to get out, but you can't. It is too deep and too steep. Your hands are broken and bleeding and you still can't get out. You finally fall flat on your back totally exhausted and with the last of your strength I see you raise your hand up toward heaven and the hand of God comes down and pulls you out of the pit."

On the Monday night after my trip to A.A. and my sense of having been totally healed, Peg and I attended our regular prayer meeting at St. Mary Magdalen Parish. That night I got up before everyone and told them God had healed me of alcoholism.

Many believed. Some did not—because they couldn't believe that Henry—the Catholic journalist, the friend of Sister Briege, the husband of Peggy and the father of such wonderful children—could be an alcoholic.

However, it was true.

The next morning, after prayer and my regular Bible reading, I set the closed Bible down on the kitchen table and started to walk away. Suddenly I said out loud, "I feel like another Psalm." I flipped open the Bible and it opened to Psalm 40, and I read: "I waited and waited for Yahweh. At last he has stooped to me and heard my cry for help. *He has lifted me out of the horrible pit!*"

There! Confirmation! My first experience of God speaking to me so directly through scripture.

This experience, too, has been part of my regular teaching. I know of alcoholics who are now sober because of my story. Alcoholics Anonymous is a great organization, a great spiritual force. But the Lord does not want me to be anonymous. I am public about my alcoholism and my healing.

I always, however, urge problem drinkers to go to A.A. It's the best program around to help people achieve sobriety.

Thank God for A.A.

As I grew stronger in faith and in self-respect after I stopped drinking, it became quite clear to me that I was sober because I at last was convinced that I was loveable. It was Peg's steadfast love through those twenty-two years of drinking that led me to sobriety. It was reflecting on that love that helped me understand that if she loved me so much I must be loveable, and that if she, a mere human, could love someone who had so wronged her, then God, who is perfect, most surely loves me too.

It was through our marriage, through human love, through the Sacrament of Matrimony more than anything else that I was healed of alcoholism.

Faith, as small as a grain of sand, and love, kissed by the Spirit in sacramental marriage, was enough for God to work with.

In the next chapter, I want to talk about prayer, sin, the presence of evil. It is in coping with evil that people often feel powerless and therefore hopeless, caught in the middle between God and Satan, good and evil. But remember that The Middle is a sacred place, a holy place.

Chapter 5

FINDING GOD IN THE MIDDLE

Maybe your "big sin" isn't alcoholism. Maybe your "big sin" is underpaying your employees for the sake of a greater profit. Perhaps you refuse to promote an employee because she is a woman.

Maybe your big problem is adultery or masturbation. Maybe your "big sin" is selling drugs, even to minors.

Everyone sins. Sin is real. Sin is as obvious as sexual abuse of children and pornography, or it is as subtle as a doctor raising his fees when he doesn't have to do so.

Sin can seem harmless—such as cheating on college tests or stealing a hundred dollars from a millionaire, or it can be obviously harmful—as in the case of rape, murder and war.

Maybe you are basically a moral person but you are angry with God because your child died or your marriage failed.

Perhaps your "big sin" is an unforgiving heart. Maybe your unmarried daughter got pregnant. Maybe you can't forgive her.

Perhaps you are angry with God because you are suffering from cancer or have been crippled or badly burned. Maybe you lost your job—and subsequently lost your dream home and your dream wife.

It is not a sin, always, to be angry with God. Anger is an emotion and that emotion expressed honestly to God is a move in the right direction. Just don't hide from God. Don't give him the cold shoulder. Tell him you are mad as hell at him. He's a big boy. He can take more than we can dish out—and he loves honesty. He can work with an honest person. What grieves God is a liar or a person who runs away from him.

Sin seems rather tame to most people. But sin, evil itself, can take on terrifying proportions.

It is a terrifying experience to see a person oppressed or possessed by evil spirits. I am not an exorcist. I don't even have a reputation for being a good "pray-er" for healings and for delivering people from spiritual bondage to evil spirits. But I have witnessed one such deliverance.

I saw the paralyzing agony of a woman moving from devil worship to worship of the one true God.

Her experience, shared here, should serve to put sin, as evil, in proper perspective. For all sin is evil, even if it isn't always as frightening as was this case.

The woman in question, we'll call her Alice, came to a prayer group one evening. She had been given a Bible by a mechanic. The woman seemed frightened. She drew away from everyone who approached her.

Eventually, the prayer group leaders learned that this woman was making an effort to come into the Church but that she had a tremendous obstacle to overcome. As a child, Alice had been consecrated to Satan. She had been a Satan-worshiper and had participated in all sorts of evil.

Some people would like me to say that she was prayed over and instantly healed. She was not instantly healed.

Alice did her best to fit into the group—but most people, good Catholics and Christians all—were afraid of her, afraid to be contaminated by Satan, afraid to touch or hug the woman. They did hug her, but it was swift, stiff, formal, tentative, conditional.

One woman in the prayer group, however, took a personal interest in Alice. She befriended Alice, prayed with her, ate with her, visited her. We'll call this woman Betty.

Betty made herself available to Alice—night and day, anytime when Alice felt oppression, fear, uncertainty, when the utility company was ready to cut off her electricity, when her children were sick, Alice would call Betty.

Over many, many months, Betty and Alice met, prayed, talked, laughed and cried together. Alice continued attending prayer meetings, began going to Mass. Through Betty's love and ministry, Alice found acceptance. In that human acceptance, she found Jesus.

Alice was baptized in the parish church and the entire prayer group attended. Having witnessed the slow and painful healing, the undying hope in Alice, as well as Betty's steadfast love, the prayer community better understood the mystery of healing and God's way of healing. And the prayer community danced and sang all through the church the night Alice was baptized. It was a great experience—Christians experiencing overwhelming spiritual joy so that dancing and shouting and singing in the aisles became true and beautiful praise and worship.

As I have written elsewhere, "The beauty about God's forgiveness is that it is given really before it is sought. And the tragedy is that so many people, in failing to seek it, reject what is already given." The Father's redeeming love was present even before Jesus came. God does not change. But in Jesus, that love was enfleshed, personified, concretized, unmistakably offered to all people and to each person. Jesus is the greatest statement that God has always offered his forgiveness.

I don't care what a person's sin is—what spiritual or physical sickness. There can be healing, forgiveness, wholeness, even for a sin so great as worship of Satan. If God could forgive Alice, do you think for a moment he cannot, will not forgive you of your "big sin"?

God is good. Could an evil power create a sunset, a rose, a wild flower? Could an evil God create the splash of glory of New England trees in the fall or the crystal brilliance of the Rockies on a sunny winter day or the lush life of a tropical rain forest? Could an evil God create a baby's smile or a mother's embrace?

No.

God is good. When man and woman came into being, God made them in his own image. This is his word.

He made them like himself—creative, loving, beautiful, life-giving.

When man and woman forgot God, they began to reach beyond themselves, forgot they were creatures of God and tried to be equal to God. Sin came into the world.

Sin is not so much the act of adultery, the act of stealing or masturbation or violence or hatred. Sin is the very notion that the individual is the center of creation, that what the individual wants, regardless of the cost to others, is all right.

That is idolatry. It makes a god of self.

A young man came to me once. The young man, we'll call him Bob, had recently moved to Orlando. He and his girl friend, we'll call her Mary, were living together.

Bob and Mary were the typical, beautiful young couple deeply in love. But they were unhappy. Something was missing. Mary had been brought up in a strict Baptist home. Bob was Catholic. They knew and accepted in principle the Christian view of sex and marriage; they knew scripture. But they were living together and had not been married.

Bob came to me because he had read an article I had written on forgiveness.

He really wanted to know the Lord. He wanted to live life more fully.

Bob's and Mary's story is typical of so many young people who live together and express their love sexually but who do not want to marry because they are "not ready" or "not sure" or "can't yet afford to set up house."

See how subtle Satan is! The couple is living together, sharing expenses, pooling resources, breaking bread and making love— precisely what married couples do—but they cannot get married because they are "not ready" or "not sure" or "can't afford to set up house."

They profess love and commitment but refuse to formalize that commitment in a legal or religious way. They want to leave themselves an out because, really, they are not sure about marriage. They want the pleasures and intimacy of sex but do not want to tie themselves down with the commitment that sex and intimacy signify.

Such a relationship is a lie.

Bob and I spoke for many hours over the next month or so. He and Mary eventually decided on their own to live apart and prepare for marriage. They were married in the Church and now have a child. A more beautiful couple and family you have never seen.

Here was a case in which two good Christian people were trying to find happiness apart from God. Their own physical and emotional needs, their own love and attraction to each other pushed aside their sense of balance, of right, of subordination to God and his way, and they began to seek happiness in themselves. The relationship could have been a disaster. Before marriage, while they were together, there was increased bickering. Mary was more and more insecure because she really wanted to be married; Bob was more and more frustrated by her insecurity that he felt would make unreasonable demands on him forever after.

They were playing at love. There is no love without commitment—only infatuation, only physical and emotional passion and release. Without commitment, there can be no spiritual satisfaction. With commitment, sexual love brings spiritual passion as well as physical, the thrilling fulfillment of the total person, the ultimate experience in what it means to be fully man, fully woman and fully together.

To work against our nature, to demand fulfillment without fully giving all we have to give, is sin. It is sin because it is selfish. Sin destroys individuals and therefore relationships.

It is tempting to discuss only sexual sins when we talk about sin. Sexual sin is so prevalent today—but not more prevalent than injustice.

And, unfortunately, there are grave injustices in the Church. There are injustices against women, against blacks, Hispanics and Haitians, against children and old people. Sometimes it is difficult to see where the world ends and the Church begins.

Oh, yes, in the Church there are injustices, there is sin. When investments are more important than ministries to the poor and to refugees, when priests and lay ministers hesitate to learn other languages to minister to refugees and immigrants, when women are paid less and refused promotions because they are women, when lay employees are underpaid and overworked, when priests and congregations hate one another, when ministers forget the spirit of service and make themselves such a center of adulation that God is shoved into second place, there is sin in the church.

There is sin in the White House, in Congress, in the state legislatures and in the voting booth when the poor are denied their fair share of the nation's wealth. There is sin in the family when parents refuse to forgive their children and lead them gently home to their forgiving and loving Lord.

There is sin everywhere—but grace is everywhere, too.

Bob and Mary wanted out of their unhappiness. They found the Lord in the midst of their problem. They solved their problem when they admitted their need, looked for him, found him and obeyed him.

He is a good Lord. He does not make selfish demands. His Commandments are based on love, not on a sick need for power over people, not on delight in suffering. He made us in love. His Commandments are the "blueprint" he used in making us. His Commandments are meant to help us become fully what we can become—sons and daughters of God who shine with his very glory.

"Don't have strange gods," the Lord says, "because that will separate you from me, the source of life. And don't hate your neighbor because that's the same as hating me. Remember, I created each of you, all of you. I love each of you, all of you. Do not hate what or whom I love.

"Honor your parents because they are the avenue through which I have called you into being and honoring them connects you with me."

The Lord says we are not to commit adultery because adultery is taking what belongs to another. The Church, examining the meaning of that Commandment, sees it extending into premarital relations, into homosexual relations. Illicit sex of any kind weakens people and undermines the power of individuals and of the race to express love and commitment. It threatens family life that should be the foundation of an ordered society and the basis for both continuance and support of the human race.

The way out of The Middle, out of temptation, out of sin is Jesus. Jesus came and showed us our holy destiny through his resurrection and ascension. He then sent the Spirit—and it is this Spirit who gives life, who instructs.

It is the Spirit who makes God present in The Middle of pain, frustration, temptation, suffering and oppression. The Spirit moved Betty who had been nourished by Word and Eucharist, and she was able to help Alice who was suffering captivity in the kingdom of darkness.

The Spirit is alive. He has power. He empowers Christians. Pentecost is today as well as two thousand years ago. Pentecost comes with baptism, with confirmation, with all the sacraments. It is impossible to receive Jesus without receiving the Father and the Spirit, too. Jesus said that he and the Father would come to those who believe in him and make their "dwelling place" with him (John 14:24). He said, "I will ask the Father and he will give you another Paraclete—to be with you always: the Spirit of truth . . ." (John 14:16-17). And he also said of the Spirit, ". . . the Holy Spirit, whom the Father will send in my name, will instruct you in everything" (John 14:26), and the Spirit "will bear witness on my behalf. You must bear witness as well, for you have been with me from the beginning" (John 15:26-27).

The Spirit is at the heart of Christian life. Without the Spirit, there could be no Eucharist, for at Mass the priest begs the Father to let the Spirit come upon the bread and wine "so that they may become the Body and Blood" of Jesus.

There can be no Christian without the Spirit. It is the Spirit who signs a person with the sign of the Cross, the Spirit who sanctifies, who transforms with his powerful and sevenfold gifts.

It is the gifts of the Spirit, those transforming gifts from Isaiah 11:1 and following that turn pagans into Christians: Fear of the Lord, Piety, Fortitude, Counsel, Knowledge, Understanding and Wisdom. These were the gifts Mother Angelica asked God to give me in that powerful prayer during our first meeting.

Her prayer has already hinted at what these magnificent transforming gifts do for us. But if we are to understand more fully the importance of living in the Spirit of God, we should consider them more carefully and frequently pray for the Spirit to fill us with these gifts. I want to describe briefly what each of these gifts provides so we can see clearly how God is in The Middle, each Middle, your Middle and my Middle.

1. *Fear of the Lord* gives us a sense of God's greatness. Through the Spirit's wisdom, we realize that God is Creator and we are creatures. Once, at prayer, I meditated on my creatureliness. Suddenly I found myself in front of the Creator. I was a nothing standing

before this great Something and I wanted to be something-in-Something. I just let Something assimilate me. It was almost like osmosis, and when I was assimilated there was nothing but light and peace. I couldn't see Something, but he was there, very much there, all around me, and in me.

I call God "Something" not to be irreverent but out of necessity. When, in that spiritual exercise, I saw him with my spiritual eyes, he had no name, no shape, no substance. He simply was—and I was utterly dependent and subject to him, unable to know him, not wanting, really, to know him but desiring deeply to be with him, in him, of him, for him.

That is the gift of Fear of the Lord. With that gift, a Christian can be poor in spirit, can begin to live Jesus' blueprint for a happy life, the Beatitudes.

2. *Piety* is not what I first imagined it to be—a special help from God to be able to pray well or without distraction. Those things are the fruit of piety. Piety is the gift of right relationship. It is the gift of love. If God is my God and your God, we have the same Father who loves us both. If he loves you, how dare I not love you? To hate you would be to call God a liar, to tell him his judgment about you is wrong, that you are not loveable. To hate you would be to set myself up as God. Piety helps us treat others as we want to be treated.

3. The Spirit gives us strength through the gift of *Fortitude*—the strength needed to overcome fear in the face of martyrdom. Fortitude also gives us the strength to overcome shyness and that destructive sense of guilt and unworthiness that keeps us from ministering to others. Fortitude is living in the strength of God himself.

Fortitude also helps us persevere in good works. How often have we heard people say, "Why don't you give up on that character. He'll never change!" But something in you says, "No. I won't give up. There is hope." That is Fortitude.

4. The gift of *Counsel* helps Christians speak with confidence to a friend in need. Counsel gives us the meaning of scripture in every situation. The Spirit, through this gift, puts wisdom within our grasp. When the Spirit whispers the Word into our ears, we come to know ourselves better. We see ourselves in the light of Jesus. We see how he is merciful in his treatment of us and we learn to be

merciful to others. Counsel unites us to God's Word and will and teaches us discernment. We can see clearly what is and what is not God's will for us.

5. *Knowledge* helps us, as Mother Angelica said, to know the one thing that counts, the glory of the Father and the good of our neighbor—and the two are one. Knowledge of God helps us detach ourselves from worldly goods, from unhealthy dependency on others. We can see ourselves in the light of Jesus. We see our brokenness, our need to depend on him. We see his mercy and we place all our hope in him. This gift of Knowledge also gives us the ability to see God in everything. Through the power of the Spirit, we *know* God is always with us, regardless of all evidence to the contrary.

6. *Understanding* is the ability to know with certainty that "God loves me" with the intensity of his love for Jesus. He cannot divide or limit himself. As he is to Jesus, so he is to us—our loving, powerful Father. Understanding gives us the light we need to penetrate the mysteries of faith, to believe that Jesus is really present in a little wafer of bread, to believe that God loves us and lives in us, to believe and to know with all our hearts that good can come out of misfortune, even out of sin, if we only trust God and flee to him with grateful, repentant hearts.

Understanding helps us approach the Lord, simply and trustingly, knowing that Jesus would die for me if I were the only person in the world. Understanding gives us this light, this spiritual knowledge that comes to us in a mysterious way. It comes through communion, through being with God, through knowing him with our spirit.

And that brings us to Wisdom.

7. *Wisdom* is the culmination of all the gifts. With this gift we become whom we worship—Jesus the Lord. St. Paul said it first: "It is not I who lives but Christ lives in me" (Gal. 2:20). We become so filled with the Spirit that we are transformed together into the Church, the Body of Christ. We also individually are Christ to others. This is the majesty and mystery of the Spirit. Through the gift of Wisdom, we see with the eyes of Jesus, hear with his ears, love with his heart, touch with his healing hand. We experience his presence in us. We feel him, know him, see him, touch him. He is

real. There is no longer room for wondering. Wisdom is the fullness of faith, of hope, of love.

We must seek the Spirit. We find him in and through the Church. The Spirit gave birth to the Church.

Today, it is through the Church, or it is through no one, that the people hear the words of Jesus, recollect the Commandments of the Father and discover the power of the Spirit. The Church alone has been given authority and power to proclaim the Word and to make Eucharist happen. Eucharist. The Real Presence. The celebration of thanksgiving. The God-with-us sacrament of love through which Jesus becomes food of mind, soul, body, spirit, community.

It is the Church's responsibility to preach convincingly and effectively, to call people into repentance and service, to enable believers to change the world from a society of hate to one of love, to call people from self-worship to worship of the one God.

The Church, ever growing and learning, must speak to the present moment. At the moment, people do not believe in sin. Perhaps they do believe but force themselves to ignore the sin because they do not understand it.

Perhaps sin, to them, is only breaking the rules of a distant, impersonal God. Perhaps they think that God contradicts himself. To their minds, perhaps, he gives freedom and then denies freedom, the power to move ahead and then restricts power with rules of conduct. If that were all there is to God, how could anyone love him or believe him? They would only fear him.

Some people do fear God. Instead of facing the fear and themselves, they deny fear. In denying fear, they deny there is anything or anyone to fear, so they end up denying God.

Others doubt God's existence because they do not understand how God, if he is real, can let evil exist. Since they abuse their own power, they cannot understand how a real God can let people ruin his own plans. Since they have little or no respect for the rights of others, they cannot understand how God respects the rights and free will of others.

Some people see God as a mean and aggressive bully who plays "cat and mouse" with them. They think he tempts them, tries to trick them. They think he takes some kind of fiendish delight in their misery, in their struggle to be good and even greater delight when they fail to be good. They do not understand that temptation comes from Satan and not from God.

Most Christians think of temptation only as an occasion of sin. But it is more. It is also an occasion of grace. If this were not so, how could Bob and Mary have realized they were off base? How could I, always tempted to have that next drink, have known that I was in sin and needed and could find deliverance? I stayed addicted to booze for a long time. But I never stopped praying for deliverance. I could not have known I could pray if, within the temptation and the sin, my Father had not been present in me, calling me to health, wholeness and holiness.

During temptation, an invitation to do evil, there is also the invitation from God to do good. This is called grace. It is gift, the presence of the Spirit and his gifts.

Grace is always present, even when a person is in sin, even when a person has rejected God. For God is a loving and jealous God, and Jesus tells us that he wants healing for the sinner, not death.

People need the Church's help in seeing God in the midst of their temptations, troubles and sufferings. But Christian ministers often have missed the point themselves. They have failed to see God in the midst of human sin and agony. When confronted with a social evil like pornography, Christian churches immediately want to form picket lines and lobby the state legislatures or Congress.

They seek "decisive action" from congregations, the law and from lawmakers. While decisive personal and political action is needed to change social influences from evil to good, the churches must remember they can do something no one else can do—preach the Gospel. Only the churches, only committed Christians can call people into repentance through faithful and faith-filled preaching of the Word.

St. Paul deemphasized the law and spoke of faith. Laws will not get rid of social evil—only conversions will ultimately end evil.

One of the greatest sins in the Christian Church today is the slothful attitude toward proclaiming and preaching the scriptures, the lack of faith we have in the power of God's Word. God's Word is the Real Presence of Jesus just as surely as is the Eucharist!

Christian churches must begin to preach the full Gospel, not the incomplete gospel of condemnation or the dull gospel of disbelief.

Sin is more attractive than a preacher's condemnation and more powerful than disbelief. The churches must preach Jesus.

There are too many preachers advocating some sort of psychological salvation, too many preachers whose sermons disregard human participation in salvation and put the entire burden on the Lord. And there are too many preaching their own gimmicky (and profitable!) approach to wholeness and happiness, too many who are not willing to accept the Cross as part of the Good News. Crosses do not enhance profitable preaching! Jesus, however, warned that all his disciples must be willing to suffer and even die for his name.

At the same time, sinners don't need condemnation. They already have problems enough with their own unhappiness, oppression and enslavement of one kind or another. They do need hope. If they hear often enough that God loves them and if they find that love enfleshed in believers, they will perhaps themselves begin to believe.

After Vatican Council II, the Charismatic Renewal pushed the Spirit into prominence in the mainline churches. We talk, now, about life in the Spirit, about how the Spirit renews individuals and entire communities. I will go into this "life in the Spirit" in more detail later, but right now, a little story will help illustrate how important it is to have a visible, active and lively faith-community that beckons people to believe.

This is a story about a young man. We'll call him Gus.

Gus is typical of many Catholic young adults. He was a Catholic for all of his twenty years. As he entered young adulthood, he realized he was unhappy. He was having sexual experiences and he felt guilty. The sermons from the Catholic pulpit were of no help. Some fundamentalist friends took him to their church.

Through their ministry, Gus discovered the power of the Word of God. He found a community of people who openly and enthusiastically expressed faith in Jesus and who showed genuine interest in him.

They loved him, worked with him, encouraged him. Gus was the center of attention. Everytime he got an insight into the scriptures, he was cheered. They loved him enough to lead him to what they understood as salvation. They wanted him to be "born again" so he could have everlasting life.

But as so often happens, this group of believers had tunnel vision. While they said it "makes no difference which church you go to," they kept attacking the Catholic Church, they kept trying to lure Gus away from his traditional and sacramental faith.

Fortunately, Gus's fundamentalist mentor decided he was going to make even more inroads into the Catholic community and "save" even more of his peers from Catholicism. He and Gus attended a parish RENEW program. RENEW is a three-year process of spiritual growth through small-group prayer and sharing of faith.

While trying to save Catholics, the young evangelical lost Gus back to Catholicism. Gus—having seen the faith alive in his Catholic peers, having tasted the excitement of a sacramental spirituality lived with evangelical enthusiasm—is again a committed Catholic, attends Mass regularly and is a solid Christian working on his spiritual growth.

Gus found new life among the evangelicals. He found a conversion of heart that he had not personally experienced sitting in a Catholic church on Sunday. Now, back in a lively parish, Gus is sharing that conversion experience.

Gus's experience should tell Catholics something: To bring about change in individuals and societies, we must bring people to (1) conversion and (2) new life.

1. *Conversion*, a change of heart, obviously involves more than a superficial or one-time acceptance of Jesus as Lord and Savior.

Conversion is an ongoing process. We sin—even after we have accepted Jesus. So we need constant conversion, constant growth, constant repentance. That's why I preach a "spirit of grateful repentance." We are sinners covered by his blood.

But conversion begins with that initial realization that "Jesus loves me" or that "Jesus did die for me" or something like that. But people can never believe in Jesus if they never hear of him. They will never hear of him if we do not, all of us, preach him. Lay Christians must begin to share their faith more openly and with greater enthusiasm. And to do so, they will need more motivation from the pulpit. The pulpit itself must become more effective in reaching people who come to church out of fear, mere habit, simple curiosity or under parental duress.

Preachers, teachers and all believers would do well to reflect on

Psalm 137:6: "May my tongue cleave to my palate if I remember you not, if I place not Jerusalem ahead of my joy."

The psalmist is saying that if we forget God, if we forget Jerusalem (for us, the Church, the Bride of Christ, his presence with us), then we should not speak.

If preachers and teachers are not praying, if they are not reflecting on scripture, if they are not repenting and begging forgiveness, if they are not forgiving their own enemies, if they are not interceding for the people they serve, then their tongues should be stilled.

I can't preach the Good News if I do not believe it or live it. The Good News is not salvation by a distant God, but salvation by a God who took our flesh, who suffered all our temptations, who, though innocent, died at the hands of guilty people for guilty people. The Good News is a God who still lives with us, among us, in us, whose help is inherent in his presence in us.

That's good news—God is where we are, caught in The Middle: in The Middle of temptation, sorrow, pain and frustration, of the terrible whirlpool of habitual sin, drug addiction and alcoholism, of those damnable decisions that promise we will be wrong regardless of what we do.

The Sunday sermon is supposed to break open the scriptures, to reveal what they mean in human history, what they meant when they were written, what they mean to the community hearing the preaching.

If a preacher is not spending at least ten hours in prayer, study, reflection and writing for her or his homilies, that preacher's tongue should be still!

If a preacher is not spending at least an hour a day in prayer— besides Mass and scripture study—that preacher's tongue should be still! No excuse about busy schedules and people in need. Preaching is a ministry. People need good preaching just as surely as they need proper food and counseling. Preaching should have the same claim to time given to planning and executing a parish festival, fund drive or set of parish goals and objectives.

Conversion is also aided by the example of Christians who live their faith. I will discuss this subject in more detail in the chapter on evangelization (something the Catholic Church has not yet embraced and certain evangelicals have abused terribly).

2. *Change of habits.* It is not enough to say "Lord, Lord," and it is not enough to work miracles of healing. The Lord himself tells us this in Matthew 7:21 and following. To be converted is to change lifestyles, to reject Satan and his ways, to break out of habitual sin, to enter into habitual grace.

What we are about is helping people who, having accepted the Lord (having been saved), want to become his followers.

That's where the Holy Spirit comes in. Jesus said the Spirit would teach us, form us, change us.

Christians can make a difference in the world—and they can begin by living *in the Spirit* so they can work the wonders of grace in a grace-starved world.

Christians generally do not appreciate the Spirit of God, do not know how to relate to him. They know that Jesus became man, that Jesus relates to the Father and that they "see the Father" when they see Jesus (John 14).

But the Spirit is different. He emanates from the relationship between Father and Son. He is not flesh. He is not Creator or Redeemer. He is a sanctifier, a counselor, a consoler.

Most of our prayers are to Jesus or the Father, to Mary and other saints. About the only prayer we ever say to the Spirit is "Come Holy Spirit, fill the hearts of your faithful and enkindle in us the fire of your divine love. Send forth your Spirit and we shall be created and you shall renew the face of the earth."

A prayer that asks pure Spirit to send forth his Spirit. A prayer that says we are *his* faithful. A prayer that says the Spirit's love is a fire, that he creates us anew and through us renews the earth.

It is a common prayer, so common that perhaps we don't listen to it. The words have great meaning.

Christians must develop a better understanding of the Spirit and his role in the Church. To repeat what has already been said, it is so important to know, to understand, to believe that the Spirit is sent by Jesus, that the Spirit gives life and form to the Church. The Spirit instructs us, guides us and transforms us. He makes us into the Body of Jesus, and we carry on the ministry of Jesus, renewing the earth through love, healing, preaching, teaching.

A Christian cannot come to know Jesus personally without the Spirit.

Whenever someone comes to me for prayer, I always pray to the Trinity: to Father, Son, Spirit. And I throw in a prayer to Mary, the Mother of God, our precious Lady, for good measure.

A young man was discovering God after he had been arrested for possession of cocaine. He was twenty-nine years of age and had been on drugs since he was thirteen. He was facing a trial and possible prison sentence. He was caught in the middle. He was between a rock and a hard place. His wife had left him. He wasn't spending enough time with their only child, an infant son. He had lost his job, his house, his family—everything and everyone who made him who he was.

But he had not lost the Lord. He had good Christian friends, Catholics who attended our parish. They began loving him and helping him. They referred him to me.

I asked the man what he wanted from me.

He looked at me and, with a voice still trembling with anger, pain and hate, he said, "I need to know the Lord better."

We talked for a while. He was tense. I actually was afraid he would become violent, but through the anger he said again and again, "I need to know the Lord better."

After about fifteen minutes, he began to calm down. I asked him if he wanted me to help him discover the Lord who lived in his heart. He said he did. We prayed. I asked the Father in the name of Jesus to bless him, to set angels around him to guard him. I asked Jesus to bathe him in his precious blood, to save him, to call him by name. I asked the Spirit to fill him with peace, to reveal Jesus to him in a special way, to give him whatever thought or scriptural passage this young man needed to gain strength and to feel the presence of God. I asked the Spirit to give him the gift of faith and the gift of prayer.

I asked Our Lady to cover him with her protective mantle of prayer.

The man seemed renewed. Hope shone in his eyes. His hands no longer shook. His face was relaxed. He wanted to see me again. We agreed on a total of four meetings, one every two weeks.

Not everyone has this big a problem. Not everyone hits rock bottom before realizing he or she needs the Lord. But anyone who wants to know God better, to come to know Jesus personally, must accept the ministry of God's Spirit. In the remainder of this chapter, I want to talk about the Spirit and how he relates to all of us, human beings, made in the image and likeness of the Triune God.

God is Trinity. He has revealed this. We must acknowledge him as he is. And knowing him as Trinity helps us know ourselves better since we are made in the image of God. We, too, are trinitarian. Our spirit, our soul, our mind—call it what you will—has three basic powers or functions. Old theology called them three "faculties." I prefer calling them three powers.

These three powers are memory, intellect and will.

The memory resembles the Father. Through memory we can recall the past, project the future and call them both into the present moment. What a fantastic power—to be able, for example, to recall the first meeting with your husband or wife, to remember your wedding day and honeymoon, the birth of all the children, all the vacations, the sicknesses, the good times and the bad—and then, collect them all in the present moment as you plan a twenty-fifth- or fiftieth-anniversary celebration, or a family reunion, or a wake service.

The memory is indeed a precious power.

The intellect resembles Jesus, the Son. Nothing thrills me more than struggling to understand something and then to understand it. There is a certain triumph in mastering what seemed beyond understanding. That's the way it was in geometry. To work on the problems, to run possible solutions through the mind, to discover, at last, the right principle, to apply it, to see it all make sense—that is sheer joy.

But our intellect does more than that. It works with the memory in helping us gather proper data for value judgments, for making decisions. The intellect studies the scriptures, the counsel and the experiences brought forth by the memory. In 1985, more than thirty years after he had died, the words of my boyhood pastor came ringing into my ears one day. I had been musing over spiritual growth, trying to make an important decision about options open to me in ministry. I was asking God to give me some insight. It was then that I "heard" Father Verheem's voice, "Trust God. Do good. God will bless you."

Now that may seem like common spiritual advice, even rather fundamental and simple. It is. But in the midst of confusion, in The Middle of a big decision with all kinds of options and ramifications, it was the best advice possible.

I can never forget that the famous and late Vince Lombardi kept his Green Bay Packers winning each year by returning to the fundamentals. When games became tough and victory seemed impossible, Coach Lombardi went back to the fundamentals. Good tactics for spiritual training and battle as well!

The will resembles the Holy Spirit. The will makes decisions based on what the intellect knows and values.

The will is a tough one to understand. It is, according to one line of Catholic philosophy, the power to make decisions. Decision-making is surely connected to analyzing problems, but it is a different function. I know some people who simply can't make decisions. They are always afraid they will do the wrong thing. So they never do anything, and the funny thing is that to decide to do nothing is a decision in itself. Making such a decision out of fear is dangerous. Such people need to realize it is less dangerous and much more profitable to make decisions based on facts and prayer and counsel.

The will, the power to decide, is an important part of human life and human spirituality. It is the power that leads to actions, and we know that actions speak louder than words. We remember Jesus' parable (Matt. 21:28ff.) about the two sons: one said he would not go to work, but did; the other promised to work, but never did. Which one, Jesus asks, did his father's will? Decision is more than words. Action, it seems to me, is the best evidence of what decision has really been made.

We have all heard of faith, hope and charity. These are three virtues, powers or graces God gives us at baptism. They come with the Spirit—and I believe that somehow each of these is the product of one or more of the specific transforming gifts of the Spirit listed in Isaiah 11.

In 1 Corinthians 13, St. Paul tells us that there are "three things that last, faith, hope and love, and the greatest of these is love." Love endures when there is no longer need for faith and hope. In heaven, we will know God and all there is to know about him.

There will be no need for faith. In heaven, we will be fulfilled and want or need nothing. There will be no need for hope. In heaven, seeing God as he is, seeing all our loved ones and all other saints basking in divine love, we will be moved to love, and only love will last.

But these three spiritual graces, these three virtues of faith, hope and love, feed our trinitarian spirits.

Hope feeds the memory. When I am trying to minister and suddenly the devil tempts me to despair by showing me my past sins, the Lord gives me hope to combat the temptation.

For me, hope is very tangible. The Lord has given me a sign of hope. It is a small, imaginary, golden cross that suddenly plops over the recollected sin. The little cross reminds me that my sin has been forgiven, that I have been redeemed, that God has forgotten the sin and if anyone is remembering it, it is Satan and not God. Through my own little sign of hope, I can renounce Satan, claim the blood of Jesus and go on about my ministerial business.

I believe that hope is born of the Spirit's gifts of *Fortitude* and *Counsel.* When we recall the Word of the Lord and his work in our lives, when the Spirit strengthens us in times of temptation, we automatically are filled with hope.

Faith feeds the intellect. It is faith that senses the Lord's presence in all things, faith that gives us an intimate and personal knowledge of God as Father. It is faith that helps us to understand how God is present in every situation and gives foundation to our optimism and steadfastness.

Our eldest son, when he was only eleven years old, contracted Bright's disease. The doctor said he was as sick as he could get without dying. I was lying in a bed in his hospital room praying the rosary. I remember I was weeping quietly because I was so afraid my son would die.

David asked quietly, "Daddy, am I going to die?" Suddenly it was very clear to me, as though a light had been turned on in my head. David was not going to die. So I responded with full confidence, "No, son. You are not going to die."

And he didn't. Today, he is an honored career soldier in the United States Army.

Faith had told me he would not die.

The Spirit's gifts of *Fear of the Lord* and *Knowledge* are the foundation for this gift of faith, the package in which faith comes. To see God as he is puts us in awe of him; to know him as the powerful Father who is present to us in all situations lets us trust him with all our heart.

Love feeds the will. It is hard to think of love as a gift if we see love only as an emotion. Love is basically a decision. It is an act of the will. It is wanting and doing what is best for the beloved regardless of how one feels. A husband may hate to change dirty diapers —but he does so because his wife needs help and his baby is dirty. Doing it is not fun. It doesn't make him feel good. Dirty diapers don't stop stinking just because you are lovingly changing them. That kind of love is more than emotion, more than thrill. It is born in the deep recesses of the human spirit where Father, Son and Spirit live; it is Kingdom love, rooted in that communitarian and divine love of the Persons of the Trinity.

No matter that a person has not accepted Jesus as Lord. No matter that a person claims to be an atheist. People live because God holds them in existence. If they love at all, it is because he loves.

The Spirit comes at baptism with *Piety, Understanding* and *Wisdom.* These transforming gifts contain the power that enables people to love as God loves, to decide for the sake of the beloved, to do what is necessary for others. Piety lets us see others as co-equals in the Father, as brothers and sisters of the Lord. Piety gives us right relationship. Understanding is itself a gift of love, enabling the faithful one to see how pure and perfect and steadfast is God's love. Wisdom is the culmination of all the gifts, the conscious realization of the indwelling God, the awareness of his presence, his power, his goodness and mercy. "God is love," the scriptures tell us (1 John 4:16) "and he who loves abides in God and God in him."

God is Trinity. He manifests his creativity in the Person of Father, his redeeming love in the Person of Son and his sanctifying and consoling power in the Person of Spirit. He loves us so much that when we can't or won't or don't know how to pray, his own Holy Spirit, knowing our needs, groans to the Father, prays for us! God prays for us to himself when we cannot or will not pray! (Rom. 8:26). What a generous God!

We must know him and love him as he reveals himself to us.

How do we get to know the Lord better? How do we get on a "first-name basis" with Jesus? How can we really accept, in a meaningful and fruitful way, Jesus as personal Lord and Savior?

For several years, the Charismatic Renewal has been sweeping through the mainline churches in the U.S. The Catholic Church itself has been affected by this movement of God's Holy Spirit.

Not everyone in the Renewal has remained true to doctrine, to Catholic tradition, to the Church's eucharistic spirituality. But most have. And among those who have we find some of the most influential preachers, teachers and healers in all of Christianity. To name a few: Cardinal Joseph Suenens of Belgium, chosen by two popes to act as a universal pastor to the Renewal; two women I've already mentioned, Sister Briege and Mother Angelica; several outstanding priests, Fathers John Bertolucci, Michael Scanlan, Richard Rohr. And there are several great lay ministers as well: Barbara Shlemon, Diane Brown, Tom and Pam Edwards, George Martin, Charles Osburn, Bruce and Linda Simpson and many others.

These dymanic spiritual leaders all have one thing in common. They are people of prayer; their faith is centered in the Eucharist. They also all speak of normal Christianity, a Christianity in which Jesus lives with, in and among his people, a Christianity in which prayer permeates all of life and God answers prayer.

In the next chapter, I want to go into "ordinary Christianity," the Christianity of the early Church, the Christianity that can and must be ours today. We can no longer play at being Christians. The Lord is calling for commitment, for faith, trust, for laborers who are willing to share their faith with others, for Christians willing to ask him to heal, to work miracles, to bring about conversions, to heal relationships, to preserve goodness in humanity.

Many people want to be saints. You can see them silently praising God for the example of a Mother Teresa or a John Paul II. Their admiration seems to be almost a prayer to God for a similar measure of grace. These beautiful, yearning people love holiness —but they do not feel holy and do not believe, perhaps, that they can be holy. They do not have to be, cannot be, must not be carbon copies or clones of other people, even great people like the pope and Mother Teresa. Saints are people who are fully themselves in God.

Do you want to be holy? I will tell you how to become holy. It is really simple.

Pray.

Ask God to make you holy.

I abhor preachers and teachers who make people treat God like some kind of puppet on a string. Use the right number of prayers, stand on the right verse of scripture, believe with all your heart and God will just have to do what you want him to do! What a sin!

God is not a divine Santa Claus!

Yet I will promise you one thing, brothers and sisters. I promise you God will answer one specific prayer. Ask him to let you know him better, as he wants to reveal himself to you; ask him to teach you to love him and other people more fully; ask him to make you holy. I guarantee that if you utter that prayer only once, and mean it, God will answer your prayer. He will reveal himself to you. He will teach you to love him and others more fully. He will make you holy.

Just remember. He may choose to reveal himself by his seeming absence. Sister Mary José Hobday, an American Indian, once said that God is never more present than when he is absent. St. Thérèse lived in a spiritual desert, without consolation for many years. God may reveal himself to you in nothingness, forcing your faith to reach more for him, forcing your faith to stretch itself beyond human capacity—and it is then, it is there, in that Middle between darkness and nothingness, when you continue to hope and to believe when there are no apparent reasons to hope and believe, it is there that you suddenly realize you hope and believe because God is, and he is in you, even though you can't feel him emotionally. You realize that your spirit is assimilated into his, that he is your life, that you are in him and therefore cannot see him in you.

Remember, too, that the Lord sometimes reveals himself in very beautiful and inspiring ways—and then seems to go away. The memory recollects the moment; the intellect relates it to the present. The temptation is to live in the past, to make God give you the thrill of his apparent presence once again. Be careful, Christian, be careful. Moments of inspiration are gifts given for specific purposes. They may be launching pads, conversion moments, confirming actions of God's Holy Spirit to let us know we are on the right track, that a time of testing is over, that a demand for his glory will be made. The moments are precious, but they are not in themselves worthy of our faith. We do not have faith in God's gifts, in spiritual thrills. We have faith in God—and we all know that God can give and God can take away.

Many people ask: "What is the best way to pray?" They seem to believe the rhetoric of certain preachers that God can be manipulated.

The best way to pray is the way *you* pray best. Some people like to just sit and watch the sun go down. They feel God's presence in this wonderful natural experience. Others like to reflect on scripture. Some read prayers from tattered prayer books. Some pray the rosary.

There are many ways to pray. But there must be one essential ingredient in all Christian prayer —the yearning desire to be with, in and for God, to seek his will in all things because he is good and cannot want what is not right for us.

If there is any real advice to give to anyone who wants to learn to pray, it is this: Simply pray! And pray simply! Prayer is conversation with God, talking to him and listening to him. He does speak to us. We can sense his presence, feel the nudge of his Spirit toward this or that scripture, answer or work.

Once I told a thirty-six-year-old drug addict to tell God he didn't believe he existed. "Tell him," I said, "that you are not sure about him. Ask him to reveal himself to you, so you can know him. Ask him to help you. He wants what is best for you."

With surprise the man objected, "But you can't petition God!"

Here was the key. This man saw God so far away, above and apart that he was unreachable. I told him my story. Time will decide what kind of story this man will be able to tell.

Prayer is possible. It is important to pray regularly, in a regular spot. Prayer is a sacred action. Choose a sacred spot. It may be the corner of your living room or bedroom. It may be on your back porch. Some people like to pray while they are driving. (Peg prays when I drive.) But praying is something too sacred to limit only to driving time. When you are driving—or milking cows or walking the dog—there are other things besides God vying for your attention. Give God a break. Give him some prime and exclusive time.

People who are not praying regularly should not jump into a rigorous prayer schedule. Begin small. Quality is more important than quantity, but as quality of prayer grows, the Christian will want more and more prayer time. God is habit-forming. But begin small. Maybe two minutes each morning if that is the limit of your attention span, the extent of your comfort in prayer. Realize that the Lord is gentle and he is not hard to please. He is easy to get along with. He doesn't demand formal language. He doesn't care all that much about grammar. He is equally pleased with formality and informality.

What the Lord wants more than anything else is your love. He likes getting our attention. He wants to share with us our joys and successes. He wants to hear about our problems and sorrows. He lives in us and he wants us to share life with him because, after all, he is our Creator. He made us. He knows us. He loves us. He yearns for us.

The beauty and mystery of prayer is not that people can spend time with God but that God wants to spend time with people.

Read some good books on prayer. Father Thomas Greene, SJ, has three great books on prayer. *Opening to God* is the first one and helps beginners learn to pray. *When the Well Runs Dry* is another book and it helps Christians deal with spiritual dryness, with those seemingly vast deserts in which God does not show himself. The third is *Darkness in the Marketplace*. This book makes the exciting statement that lay people working in the world can be contemplative.

Contemplation is a special kind of prayer. It is a gifted prayer. Contemplation is being with God. Nothing more. In contemplation, there are no words, no movements. A person simply is, in God. It is being with God entirely for the sake of being with him. Perhaps it is a special experience of what heaven may be like.

Few people have this gift of contemplative prayer because few people are aware of it or believe they, as lay people, can be contemplative.

Most people in the world hardly ever get beyond petitioning God for this or that need or favor. Sometimes they remember to thank him. Sometimes they don't.

Some people use the scriptures and their imagination to enter into the experience of God. They place themselves in the Gospel stories, they see Jesus, as I have done, sitting with them and speaking with them.

All these forms of prayer are good. We must beg God's forgiveness for our sins, thank him for his goodness and his mercy, and praise him because he is all good and worthy of all praise.

In all things, seek his will. Surrender to the Lord. Let him be the Lord of your life.

If you have never accepted Jesus as your Lord and Savior, or if you feel you have not been as close to him as you might, there is no better time than the present to take care of the problem.

I want to pray with you right now. If we were together, I would take your hand in mine. We would pray. If we were talking on the phone, we would still pray—as so many people do every day. So, why not through the printed page?

Let's pray for an increase in love for God and one another. Let's ask the Lord to fill us with his Spirit, to renew us, to teach us to seek his will in all things, to express our faith in Jesus as Lord and Savior.

Let's pray.

Lord Jesus, I thank you for this precious moment, for these my brothers and sisters. We come to you Lord Jesus in grateful repentance. We acknowledge our sins. We rely on your mercy. Jesus you said that if we believe in you we will be saved. Jesus, right now, Lord, we accept you as our personal Lord and Savior. You died so we might live. You paid the price of our own sinfulness. You are worthy of all praise, all thanksgiving. We thank you, Jesus.

Father, in the name of Jesus, I thank you for these my brothers and sisters. I ask you Father to fill them with your Holy Spirit, to call them by name, Lord Father, into a deep, loving relationship with you in and through Jesus and the Spirit.

Lord Spirit, I just beg you, Lord, to give my brothers and sisters the beautiful gift of prayer, the wonderful gift of faith, the gifts they need, Lord, to be loving sons and daughters of the Father. Fill them with your peace, your love, your healing power.

Lord Spirit, heal the broken hearts, the angry hearts, those broken relationships. Teach my brothers and sisters to forgive. Teach

them to love their enemies and family members into the fullness of
the Church.

Lord Spirit, I beg you to flow through their entire being, through
their bodies, minds and spirits, setting them free of all oppression,
all sickness, all pain, all sin.

Thank you, Lord Father, Son and Spirit.

Mary, our Mother, I ask you please to cover them with the mantle of your prayers. Show them to Jesus and show Jesus to them,
Mary, and intercede for their healing and spiritual growth before
the Father's throne, with Jesus, your Son and our brother.

Amen!

Chapter 6

LET'S RETURN TO ORDINARY CHRISTIANITY

If you are on a fence, caught in the middle between a dynamic faith in God and a tentative intellectual acknowledgment that God may, after all, exist, I have some good news for you.

I invite you now to come down off that fence, to focus on your own Middle, to hear God calling you into a life of power, a life of goodness, a life filled with wonder, awe, beauty, thrills and excitement.

God is calling you into the fullness of Christianity, into "ordinary Christianity," not a watered-down religion that passes for true religion among people afraid of the truth, not the tentative Christianity of convenient Christians. No. God is calling you into real Christianity, the Christianity of the early Church in which dead people were raised to life, in which cripples and blind people were healed, in which conversions occured in the thousands and believers had the fullness of wisdom and the power of God in their breasts.

Christianity is a powerful religion because Jesus Christ lives. It is a powerful religion because God's Spirit enlivens believers, works through them, still to this day creating signs and wonders

Christianity is a powerful religion because God does talk to his people, as the stories of Christians everywhere and in the following pages so dramatically illustrate.

Danny (not his real name) was twenty-two years of age and had been in prison three years. He was serving time in Sumter Correctional Institution in Sumter County, Florida, about seventy miles east of Orlando.

Danny was a tall, easygoing black. He was serving time for car theft or some such felony. I remember, though, that his was not a crime of violence.

I had been ministering at the prison for some months. Whenever possible, I would bring a priest from the Orlando area to celebrate Mass for the Catholic inmates. When a priest could not come, which was often, I brought Communion and we had a Communion service.

Danny, though a Catholic, never went to Communion.

One day he asked to see me privately. As we sat in the chaplain's office, Danny talked around a lot of subjects but finally said, "Henry, I sure would like to know more about the Eucharist. I want to learn more and more about my faith."

I talked to Danny for six weeks about the Eucharist. He showed great interest. I wondered why he was not going to Communion but I didn't ask. Long ago I decided that people, prisoners or otherwise, had a right to their privacy and, especially with prisoners, it is better not to ask too many questions. As they get to know you better, they'll tell you what they want you to know. The rest doesn't really matter. Ministry there, as anywhere, is loving and meeting needs, while hoping to help the listener find the Jesus within.

On our sixth visit together, after our private session, we walked into the chapel and Danny announced, "Hey, you guys, I'm going to Communion today—and it's my first time!"

"Oh, my gosh," I thought, "his first Communion! What right do I have to give this man his first Communion? What do I do?"

The eighteen or twenty Catholic inmates were crowded around Danny, thumping him on the back, congratulating him and asking me if I didn't think this was a wonderful thing.

Talk about caught in the middle!

After long months of overcoming the damage anti-Catholic prejudice had done to these Catholic inmates, after long months of talking about God's love and the strength, wisdom and consolation, to say nothing of forgiveness, that comes from the sacraments, especially the Eucharist, I could hardly refuse to give this man Communion.

On the other hand, my *Baltimore Catechism* serving me well, I knew this man had not gone to confession and he was not in prison for praying the rosary.

What to do?

I made a pastoral decision.

Do you know what a pastoral decision is?

It's doing what you want to do and hoping you don't get caught!

I decided to give Danny his first Communion.

After the scripture readings, I led Danny through the Act of Contrition, the Act of Faith and I led him through an act of faith in the real presence and had him commit himself publicly, to his fellow inmates, that he would try to serve Jesus well.

Danny made his first Communion and there was great joy in the chapel that day.

Back home in the parish, I told my pastor about my problem and decision and he said I had done the right thing.

That isn't the end of the story. The next week, I went to the prison and there was no Danny. "Where's Danny?" I asked.

"He couldn't make it today," responded Tom, the inmate who was leading the Catholic inmates in scripture studies and encouraging attendance at Catholic services.

The next week, there was still no Danny. "Oh, Danny's tied up this week."

I thought it strange, but prisons are strange places.

During the following week I spoke with a nun from Tampa who visited the same prison. She asked me, "Have you heard what happened to Danny?"

I said I hadn't and she told me that the week after he received his first Communion, he was stabbed several times with an ice pick. He had taken on five inmates who were trying to rape a young man who had just arrived at the prison.

I wondered why Tom hadn't told me about Danny, but I supposed he had his own reasons.

The very next day I got a letter from Danny. He told me about the stabbing, but he told me something far more significant to him, to me and to this discussion of the Eucharist.

Danny said that while he was in the hospital section of the prison, he discovered a way to escape. He made plans to escape. He
wanted to escape very badly, because in the hospital room, he could
look out his window "and see birds come and eat my crumbs and
then fly away. And in the distance I could see free people driving
their cars along the superhighway. And, Henry, I wanted to be free.

"The day I was going to escape, I suddenly realized I was in prison because I had always run away. I realized that if I started running again I may never be able to stop running. So I fell on my
knees and asked Jesus to come into my life.

"He did. And we sat down on the bunk and talked together.

"Henry, I will never ever again be afraid. I forgive all who have
hurt me and ask forgivenenss from those I have hurt. I will never
ever again be afraid."

Danny loved with a great love. He received his Lord and found
the strength to risk his life to help a total stranger. He rescued the
young man from shame, pain and disgrace. He rescued him, probably, from a life of forced prostitution. Danny was stabbed for his
trouble.

But he will never be afraid again.

That is the strength, the power of the Eucharist. To receive the
Eucharist is to receive the Lord, to be filled with the Lord's goodness, strength and love

This is ordinary Christianity, the kind of Christianity through
which disciple and Lord come together for intimate conversation,
for communion, for a taste of what heaven is all about. The Eucharist is ordinary Christianity.

Since I began again to go to daily Masss—about eight years
ago—the Eucharist has become the central reality of my life. My
story is not as dramatic as Danny's. Yours may be more dramatic,
but each of us, receiving the Lord in faith, receives his grace. Our
lives are changed. We grow in wisdom.

I know my spiritual growth, my increased faith and my excitement over the Lord is due in large part to prayer. The Lord instructs us as we pray. I try, but don't always succeed, to spend an
hour in prayer each morning before Mass and then maybe fifteen
minutes in evening prayer. I pray the rosary, the Liturgy of the
Hours, and often try to spend some time reading the Bible.

Sometimes, I pray in the middle of the night—as do many, many other Christians who have decisions to make, whose Middle is especially tense or demanding.

But the greatest gift from the Lord for spiritual growth is the Eucharist.

Of course, Eucharist is much more than receiving Communion. The Mass is Eucharist, from the Greek word meaning thanksgiving.

A retreat director once gave a meditation on the Last Supper as Eucharist. He said, "Jesus, at the Last Supper, when he instituted the Eucharist, was giving thanks. He was saying 'Thank you, Father' for his life, for his disciples and for his ministry. Jesus knew he was facing terrible torture and death, desertion by his friends and apparent failure in his mission—and in the face of that agony, Jesus said, 'Thank you, Father.'"

Everytime we celebrate the Eucharist, we enter personally into the very mystery of redemption.

Pastor Max Thurian, a Lutheran monk who is a member of a famous monastery in Taizé, France, wrote a book called *Eucharist as Memorial*. A very good friend pointed this book out to me. I want to share, in my own words, what I learned from just one chapter in Pastor Thurian's work.

Jesus was celebrating Passover as a Jew. He was a Jew. He believed as a Jew. When the Jews celebrated their deliverance from Egypt, they did not simply recall some historical, religious event. No, the Jew's faith says that even today when the Passover is celebrated, the contemporary Jew is delivered.

That is what memorial meant to the Hebrew in the Old Testament. They remember the Passover in an active, participating way. That is what Jesus was about whenever he celebrated Passover.

However, on this night, on this Passover, Jesus did something different. He took bread and wine. He said, "This is my body to be given for you. Do this as a remembrance of me ... This cup is the new covenant of my blood, which will be shed for you."

What a revolutionary statement. Either Jesus is the Son of God or he deserved death for blasphemy.

He is saying, from this Gospel of Luke (22:19-20), that whenever Passover is celebrated his followers will remember him and his new covenant as they had previously remembered Yahweh's covenant with Moses.

He is saying his covenant replaces the older covenant. He is saying that he is not only the new Moses, but someone greater than Moses, who is equal with the Father.

In faith, as we "remember" or "memorialize" the Last Supper, we are at the Last Supper, we are on Calvary, we are at the empty tomb. We do not simply recollect the event. The event, through the presence of Jesus in his Church, occurs for us. It is the same event. Jesus is in eternity. Whatever happened to him in time is eternally present to the Father. The Mass lets us "plug into" that eternal reality, so to speak, and we are present with Jesus in the upper room. We see John lay his head on Jesus' chest. We see Judas slink away. We see Jesus break the bread and bless the cup. We hear Jesus say, "This is my body ... this is my blood."

How can Catholics stay away from the Eucharist if they realize what it means? Daily, yes daily, we can come to the upper room, to Calvary, to the empty tomb. Daily we can receive from the hands of Jesus his body, his blood.

How can people attend Mass with such apathy, such lack of interest? How can some priests go through the Eucharist as though it were only a dress rehearsal for some stage play? How can readers just read words and singers be satisfied with less than everything they can give the music ministry?

Liturgies are bad because Catholics really do not believe, or at least do not understand, what they are about in Eucharist. If they did believe, they would demand better liturgies—and those who do understand are shopping around for parishes with good liturgies.

Perhaps apathetic Catholics simply do not understand that in the Eucharist they are united, through the Spirit, to the offerings going to the Father, that all their pain and sacrifices, their disappointments and their successes and joys become one with the offering, Jesus, to the Father.

Jesus makes up for our own shortcomings. He is the perfect sacrifice—because as priest he offers himself without reservation, without sin, without hesitation to the Father. He embraces his Passion for our sake, for the sake of his beloved brethren—and he loves so much that he wants all people of all generations to be able to be with him at Eucharist as he offers himself in the form of bread and wine to the Father.

Jesus stands before the Father and through the Mass gathers all of us up with him and says, "Thank you, Father."

He looks into the eyes of the Father as he holds each of us in his arms and says, "Father, I died for this one ... and this one ... and this one ..." until he has shown the Father each of us. And he does this over and over again, as long as we keep coming, as long as we let him take us in his arms before the Father's throne.

How can we not sing in praise and thanksgiving? How can we not dance in joy? How can we restrain ourselves at the greeting of peace? Don't we believe that he is there, with us, among us? Don't we believe that we have the power to give his peace to one another? Are we going to hoard his love in our own little hearts and smother it until nothing but cold ashes remain?

How terribly ungrateful are priests and congregations that simply go through the motions of the Mass. When Jesus comes again, will they be able to recognize him? Will they be able to express joy when they see him?

I don't mean that everyone in church has to be emotional or become physical. People can express joy, love and faith in a quiet way, but however they express it, it is contagious. People see it, want it, look for it, begin a journey to the Lord. Ordinary Christianity makes people say, "See how those Christians love one another!" Ordinary Christianity calls people into an appreciation of their Middle, helps them find meaning and the Lord right where they are.

I've worshiped in many churches around the nation and believe me, I can understand why some people become so frustrated that they feel they must leave the Church, although I disagree that they have to leave.

In Atlanta, I went to Mass in an historic church and heard a twenty minute appeal for money while the priest insisted he wasn't preaching for money

In Philadelphia, I heard a forty-five minute rambling "homily" that complained about liberals and mentioned no less than three times that white-tailed deer were within the city limits of Philly. So much for inspiration!

In another city, I heard a priest begin a sermon about the Good Shepherd with a personal experience of being lost in the mountains in a dense fog. It was only the voice of a shepherd, calling out to him, that led him down the mountain safely. Then he spoiled it all by going into a tirade against women libbers and homosexuals.

We all have bad days. Every parish sometimes has a bad liturgy—and even in bad liturgies the Lord comes. He makes Eucharist happen, not us, although it is our faith that calls him to come, to make it happen.

The point is that the Eucharist is our most important experience as Catholic Christians. We should worship well.

Moreover, I think people need to spend more time praying before the tabernacle. Most of my insights, my answers come in such prayer. It was before the Blessed Sacrament that I learned to forgive, that I was healed of guilt and learned that I am a sinner covered with his blood.

Sister Briege gets many, many inspirations as she prays three hours every day before the Blessed Sacrament.

Mother Angelica and her handful of nuns began and are maintaining the world's only Catholic TV satellite network—because they pray hours upon hours before the Lord in the Blessed Sacrament—and because they reflect daily on the Word of God.

Ordinary Christianity is centered both on Eucharist and Word.

I am known as a Catholic charismatic. And I admit it. I (horrors) pray in tongues and have experienced what is called the gift of Knowledge. Praying in tongues is praying, through the action of the Holy Spirit, in a language completely unfamiliar to you. It is the most misunderstood gift among all the ministerial gifts of the Spirit mentioned in 1 Corinthians 12:1 and following.

The gift of Knowledge is a gift of spiritual insight. Sister Briege has this gift in abundance.

While I am charismatic, I realize that owing to lack of pastoral involvement, some individual charismatics have become confused. These individuals, really few in number, seem more interested in the gifts than in the Giver and seem to confuse personal opinion with revelation.

As my public-speaking ministry expanded, it became very clear that I had a ministry within the Church. I was not being asked by anyone to set up large public rallies. Invitations to speak came from parishes and from Catholic prayer groups—and they all wanted to know more about Catholic spirituality, Catholic teaching, Catholic approaches to scripture.

I am terribly disappointed that so many Catholics have run away from the Charismatic Renewal. It is a gift from God sent at a time when the Church needs to rediscover the power of the Spirit.

It may help if I try to define a few charismatic terms and put them in a Catholic context. I will be referring to terms not familiar to Catholics weaned on the *Baltimore Catechism*. Theirs is a spirituality that reserved the special gifts listed in 1 Corinthians 12 to canonized saints—and celibate saints at that. St. Paul tells us that there are many gifts but the one Spirit and that to "each person the manifestation of the Spirit is given for the common good."

Earlier we discussed the personal or transforming gifts of the Spirit from Isaiah 11. Here St. Paul is talking about a different kind of gift. I call these gifts the "ministry gifts" because they are given for people to help others, not to help themselves.

The ministry gifts are as follows:

1. *Wisdom in discourse:* This gift manifests itself in at least two ways. First, it enables a person to preach with power and encourage the kind of faith that can move mountains. Scriptures come alive for those who hear this person speak or preach. People, hearing someone preach with wisdom, sense God's holy presence. The gift enhances the sense of God-with-us. Fathers Richard Rohr and John Bertolucci have this gift.

Also, this gift is called "word of knowledge." This is a gift through which God uses a person to prove his presence or to give direction. (Discernment is always needed—see below.) Sister Briege has "wisdom in discourse" or "word of knowledge" as she prays with individuals. Once she prayed with my pregnant daughter and her husband after Mass. She prayed for a healthy baby and then turned to my son-in-law and said, "Now, let's pray for that job you're looking for." Neither had mentioned a job and Peg and I hadn't either. Needless to say, the young couple felt the presence of the Lord in that encounter. They felt in a very personal way how much the Lord knows and loves them.

2. *Teaching or the power to express knowledge:* With this aid

from the Spirit, a disciple can break open the mysteries of the Christian faith as she or he shares the teachings of the Church that flow from the Word of God and tradition. The gift enables a preacher or teacher to take what has been dry theology and make it "come alive" for his or her audience. Catholics believe in the communion of the saints. What a dry and lifeless doctrine this can be if seen only in theological terms. But if a preacher can show people they are saints, in communion with all those who have gone before and are with the Lord, you have a different understanding. The communion of saints becomes one gigantic prayer meeting, a great liturgy, a time of praise, song and joy. That's teaching with power!

3. *Faith:* This is not the "gift of faith" received in baptism, but a special charism from the Spirit to make faith come alive. A person with this gift has such strong belief, such a sense of God's presence that even in very difficult situations people gain strength from the disciple's presence. In a sense, the person with this gift is, to others, an experience of God.

4. *Healing:* Sister Briege has this gift, to be sure. It is a gift, from the Spirit that helps people open up to God's healing power. The Christian does not do the healing, only the praying, only the interceding. It is the Lord who heals. But somehow the Spirit touches Sister Briege and many others in such a way that they, in praying with people, help people connect with the saving Lord who is within them

I once saw a woman healed before my very eyes. I was on a retreat with Mother Angelica in Birmingham. On Saturday evening we had a healing service. We prayed for a woman who had huge warts and a large birthmark covering most of her face. She had a huge lump on her left cheek, one of six tumors that were to be removed surgically the following Tuesday.

The next morning we had the retreat's closing liturgy. I happened to sit to the left of this woman. During Mass I actually saw the tumor on her face disappear. On Tuesday, the doctors could not find a single tumor and, Mother Angelica told me, two weeks later the woman's warts and birthmark were completely gone.

5. *Miraculous powers:* This is perhaps a rare gift, but it is a legitimate gift of the Spirit. For his own reasons, God does miraculous

things through poor human beings. Remember poor Moses in the parting of the Red Sea and getting water from the rock. A sign of miraculous powers, for example, would be making things do something that is beyond their nature—making the world stop turning, making water flow uphill, creating a spring in the desert where there is no water to be found, etc. It is easy to believe Our Lady works miracles, but we find it hard to believe that ordinary human beings can work miracles. In faith, we have to believe that all things are possible to God.

6. *Prophecy:* The gift of prophecy is not the power to predict the future, not the gift to look ahead. Rather, it is the gift to look and see within. The prophets of Israel told Hebrews the truth about themselves—they were guilty of idolatry, they were not obeying the Lord, they were vain and sinful.

The prophets were often killed for their ministry, but it is a ministry from God. God gives certain people insights into humankind's response to God, the Church's response to God. Often these people are silenced, even excommunicated or threatened with excommunication. Never does a true prophet leave the faith-community. He believes with the community and he loves the community. He may be expelled by a sinful community, but he will never leave it of his own choice.

7. *Discernment:* This word is used a lot today. "Let's pray and discern whether we should build a new football stadium, or resurface the parking lot or give $5,000 to the starving in Ethiopia." Discernment can happen both in community and in the individual pray-er. As Peg and I were praying and discerning about ordination to the diaconate, we consulted the community. The community affirmed us. God gave us peace in that affirmation. All signs said yes. That is discernment. There were no voices—although God can send visions of angels and saints or let us hear voices. But most often discernment comes through loving relationships, prayer and reflection.

When a person senses a deep peace in making a decision, that is a good sign that it is God's will.

There is, however, such a thing as "discernment of spirits." Sometimes, people experience the influence of spirits—voices or forces that seem to direct them toward this action or that. Sometimes the influences are strong and exceedingly contradictory. Sometimes the impulse is toward something suspect, like an impulse to run away from home, to sue for a divorce. One way some Christians "test the spirit" is to use a truth from 2 John 4:2-3: "This is how you can recognize God's Spirit: every spirit that acknowledges Jesus Christ comes in the flesh belongs to God, while every spirit that fails to acknowledge him does not belong to God. Such is the spirit of the anti-Christ ..."

In testing the spirit, a Christian simply asks the communicating force, "Did Jesus Christ come in the flesh?" If the answer is "yes" then the spirit can be trusted; if "no," then it cannot be trusted. Now, the Christian may not hear an actual voice but, it is said, the answer is clear to his or her own spirit. I have, on occasion, used this test and know that it has helped me in the discernment process. But I never depend only on this. I pray with and consult the community, my wife and friends. There is always the danger of the Christian becoming proud and isolating himself from community. Then he becomes the prey of the evil one.

I have a good example of how practical a gift discernment really is. It is a story of how one father, we'll call him Bill, handled the news that his unmarried daughter was pregnant.

Bill knew his children were living under terrible peer pressure and dreaded the day one of his children would become a parent out of wedlock. One day while he was at work, one of his daughters called him and asked him to hurry home, that she had something very important and serious to tell him.

Bill said that he immediately knew what the problem was. It was almost, he said, as though a small voice whispered, "This is it, Bill."

He prayed immediately, "Lord, please let me help her and love her and not hurt her and drive her away."

In his own words, Bill tells us that "by the time I had driven three blocks, I was filled with a great calm. Things began to pop into my mind. It was almost as though the Lord were whispering into my ear: 'Let her know she is loved, that she has your support, that you will help. Don't do anything to make her feel shame ...'"

When Bill entered his house and sat down, his daughter told him, "I don't want to hurt you but I am going to have a baby."

Bill's immediate response was this: "I have several things to tell you and I want you to listen carefully.

"We love you.

"You are a good person; I don't want you to feel dirty or bad about this.

"I am proud that you have the love and courage to tell us about this.

"I hope you aren't thinking about marriage simply because you are pregnant; we will help you.

"I hope you are not considering an abortion [she interrupted to say that she surely was not, that she wanted her baby].

"I want you to seek counseling to help you decide to keep the baby or put him or her up for adoption. Whatever you decide, we will support you in any way you need to be supported.

"What you have done is sinful, but I am proud of your sense of responsibility. I hope you will go to confession and get some spiritual direction. Now, what are your plans?"

For Bill, his reaction was nothing short of a minor miracle. He has a bad temper and usually flies off the handle, but he had been praying for his children, he knew the pressures they were facing, he was open to the Lord and the Lord helped him, gave him wisdom, gave him insight into the daughter's and the family's problem.

Who says God isn't with us?

8. *Tongues:* I've mentioned this gift before, but it needs a little more discussion. Why would anyone want to pray in a language he or she can't understand? Now that's a good question, a reasonable question, an intelligent question—and one that is beside the point. The gift of tongues is the gift of praise. Scripture speaks in several places about the "sacrifice of praise." Why is praise a sacrifice? Praise is saying, "Lord, you are more than me. You are bigger, better, and more intelligent. You don't need arms, legs, brains, heart or muscles. You don't need ears, or eyes or a tongue. You are complete in yourself, Lord. I want to praise you perfectly, with all my heart and soul, and even then it is not enough."

God is a good God. Remember that his Spirit groans within us, that he prays when we do not know how to pray (Rom. 8:26). That is tongues, the Spirit "groaning" within us and making melodious music in a language we do not know. But the Spirit knows what he is saying, and that is perfect prayer, perfect praise. Aware of the Spirit's ministry in us, we rejoice, our hearts say "Amen!" to what the Spirit is saying in us and through us. He is not taking away our free will. We willingly submit to his ministrations so our God can be properly praised in us. We experience great consolation to know that these poor lungs, pipes, vocal chords, this poor tongue and these poor lips are at last being used for perfect praise of God himself. What a great God!

Tongues is a great gift, a great blessing—but the proud, the cynical and the skeptical will never know it.

9. *Interpretation of tongues:* Sometimes the Spirit gives a person a prophetic message in a strange tongue. At the same time, he gives another person the gift of interpretation. I'll have to admit this sounds really strange. Why go to all that trouble? Why not just give the prophetic message in the language of the people?

I have been present when prophetic messages have been given in tongues and then were interpreted by other persons. In some cases, I knew for sure that the prophecy and the interpretation were genuine. They set well in my spirit, and people in response to the prophetic message proclaimed praise for God and lifted their voices in songs of praise. Tongues flowed through the assembly.

On other occasions, the message fell dead even before the interpretation. There is something powerful at work here. It is the Spirit of God. He sometimes may choose to use prophetic tongues and interpretation just to emphasize his message, to make sure people know it is he speaking. Always, with a true prophecy, people's spirits recognize God's voice. I like to think, too, that God enjoys his power and likes to see his children enjoying his work in them.

In that great movie, *Chariots of Fire,* the preacher who was also a runner said of God, "When I run, I can feel his pleasure." Well, when I pray in tongues, when I hear tongues of praise or prophecy and interpretations of prophesies, I can feel his pleasure.

Ours is indeed a great faith. Catholics caught in the middle of apathy or uncertainty, of unexciting faith, need only to ask the Lord to come alive in them, to make them alive in him.

Catholics who have been renewed in the Spirit must never tire of sharing their faith. Bishops and pastors must begin to make faith-sharing (evangelization) a priority. We must reach out to alienated Catholics, to the unchurched.

It is sinful that we are so hesitant about sharing our faith, so scared of the word "evangelization."

You know, God is caught in the middle. He is caught between his decision to share his Word and love through us and our own refusal to do so. One of the greatest problems in Christian churches, including the Catholic Church, is a sort of spiritual narcissism in which we serve ourselves and pamper our own spirits while we let the rest of the world live in darkness or rush head-on into hell!

But let's not blame "the Church." Lay people too easily point fingers, when they think of "the Church," at bishops and priests. But all of us together are the Church. All of us together are responsible for sharing the Word of God, for preaching the Good News of Jesus Christ.

Lay people, living in the marketplace—engineers, laborers, farmers, druggists and doctors, farmworkers, shoe salesmen, teachers, domestics—are responsible for making the Gospel present in the world. If lay people do not live the Gospel, if they do not preach with their lives and by their active outreach in faith to those who have no faith, all the King's bishops and all the King's priests will never put together this Humpty-Dumpty world.

Lay people have power—and if you are a lay person who feels powerless, I have news for you. You are not powerless. You have the ability and the grace you need to preach the Gospel in your own daily life. You can bloom fully as a Christian right where you are planted.

In the next chapter, I want to encourage Catholics who feel caught in the middle between the command to share their faith and resistance from clergy. Also, I want to talk a little about the real priestly role and ministry of the laity.

Chapter 7

POWER TO HIS PEOPLE

A friend of mine attended Mass in Atlanta—a different parish from the one I attended. The pastor, a monsignor, celebrated the Mass. He did all three readings. The altar boys brought the gifts from the back of the church at the offertory; there were no lay ministers of the Eucharist.

This was in the summer of 1986, not some time before Vatican Council II. Apparently this pastor never heard of the Council or he is disregarding it, disregarding what the Church has said about lay people becoming involved in ministries—including liturgical ministries.

Such clericalism is a sin against the Church, a sin against the priesthood of the People of God. Many lay people have been renewed in the Spirit through Cursillo, Charismatic Renewal, Marriage Encounter and other good spiritual-growth movements. When these lay people have inspired pastoral leadership they become great disciples of the Lord, active workers in the parish family, enthusiastic sharers of the Catholic faith and of the Gospel of Jesus.

These lay people, involved in the liturgies, form a bridge between celibate clergy and the rest of the people of God who live and work in the world, whose ministry of evangelization and purification of society is recognized in liturgy only through lay lectors, musicians and eucharistic ministers.

117

There are lay people, however, who have met nothing but rejection. Surely, some of these lay people lacked proper understanding of our hierarchical Church, did not appreciate our traditional, sacramental spirituality. Surely some of them developed an arrogant spirit and drove their pastors to utter frustration.

Just as surely, some of these renewed Catholics were seen by their unrenewed pastors as a threat to pastoral position and power.

Pastoral rejection is a tough test, but it is a test of the spirit of the laity. If lay people have left the Church, if they have found teachers to tickle their ears, if they have failed to meet the Lord in others in the community, they may well admit an attitude problem.

I know some Catholic lay people, too, who are completely blind to the power of the Spirit in the Catholic Church. Because priests don't run around the altar waving a Bible in the air, perspiring heavily and shouting "Jee-hee-zu-usss," these Catholics don't believe the priests really have accepted the Lord as personal Savior, really do not have the Spirit as their teacher.

I mention these clerical and lay extremes here to acknowledge their existence. I want, however, to ignore them, because a special ministry of healing is needed in each of these cases. While the problem with the majority of Catholics would be apathy rather than rebellion or disenchantment, the growing phenomenon of people opting for other churches is cause for concern.

Most often, I believe pastors want to be open to those lay people in their parishes who are willing to work, to learn and to help the mission of the Church.

I know some pastors who are truly supportive of lay people but do not believe the primary role of the laity is best expressed in liturgical ministries.

What then is the problem?

The problem, as I see it, is twofold: (1) there is still confusion over what, precisely, is the Church; and (2) because of this confusion, no one is really sure of what everyone is supposed to do to be Church and do what Church must do.

1. *Confusion over the identity of the Church.* In spite of everything said in and since Vatican Council II about the Church being the "People of God," most people in the Church still view the Church as a closed society of celibate males.

When people hear "Rome" speak of the Church, people usually think of the institutional Church, the Church of authority, the ruling, teaching Church. I am afraid that's because "Rome" thinks "hierarchy, institution, authority" when it speaks the word "Church."

People sense what Church officials mean when they try to speak of this mystery of Church.

Yet, some Catholics, when their pastor or parish council president says "Church," may well think of something other than authority and institution and hierarchy. They may think of a loving and faith-filled community.

Jesuit Father Avery Dulles in 1974 wrote a magnificent book called *Models of the Church.* He speaks of how people see the Church in different ways. Some see it as an institution; others, a sacrament or a herald of the Good News; others, as a community and still others as a servant of the poor.

The priest's point was that the Church is all of these—an institution (with organization, hierarchy, authority, clear lines of responsibility), a sacrament (the presence of Jesus in the world today), a herald (the force that proclaims the salvation of Jesus in each generation), a community (a gathering of believers who have real love one for the other), and a servant (a Church that is given to the service of the poor, oppressed and otherwise needy).

Intellectually, it is easy to agree with Father Dulles that the Church is really a combination of all these models, these elements of what I call "expressed Christianity."

But on the local level as well as in Rome, the Church becomes mainly what the pastor, parish staff and lay leadership experience it to be.

This is not the result of a malicious move to control all the other people in the parish. Rather, it is the result of people living their faith, sometimes without challenging their basic concepts and priorities.

That's why it's vitally important for ministers in the Church, as well as other leaders, to stay in touch with the "mind of the people," the "pulse of the parish," the "dynamics of dialogue."

A parish can call itself a community but still have dead worship and no real collegial processes. Calling a parish a community does not make it a community.

Likewise, a parish can say it serves the poor and do a lot of talking about serving the poor and never really make the poor a budgetary priority; or a parish can say it is the presence of Jesus in the world while, in reality, it is full of factions, squabbles and self-interest. And so on.

I am afraid that in most parishes, when priests and people say "parish," they are speaking really of only two dimensions of Church —the organized parish structure (institution) and the community (all those smiling faces who gather to share the joy of being Christian). These parishes may well have some outreach to the poor, to the bereaved, to the jobless. But by and large, the parish sees itself as separate from the world—because it has such unique concerns, because it can operate like a well-oiled machine within a vacuum and, to some degree, because its principal minister is usually separate from the world, a man (with rare exception) and a celibate (with rare exception).

This is a far cry from what the early Christians experienced. They had no church buildings, no parish structures. Their parish was the world; their congregation, anyone who happened to be willing to listen to the marvelous news that humankind had been redeemed by a Savior risen from the dead and that this Savior would come again to establish the Father's Kingdom for his chosen people.

With all good intentions, from Rome to St. Economy Parish in Fast Buck, State of Well-Being, we have basically an institutional concept of Church. We speak of the People of God, but when we do, we see these People of God sitting in church, or in cell groups, scripture study, CCD classes, pre-Cana instructions, in RCIA and in booths at parish festivals. We see "People of God" under the pastoral (and often paternal) eye of a benevolent pastor, who calls his flock to be Church *outside* the world.

We do not so easily see "Church" and "People of God" in Catholics as they live and work in the world.

It's not planned that way—that's just the way it is, given our history over the last four hundred or so years, when lay people depended on priests for everything because the laity were not expected to read and understand scripture. Priests were the only ones with an education.

I have high hopes that this is changing. I know a lot of people —laity, priests and bishops—who truly want it changed.

I am reminded of St. Paul who continued to work as a skilled laborer throughout most of his ministry. He preached a powerful Gospel by that dedication to labor—just as Jesus did in his so-called "hidden life," that part of his life from boyhood to the beginning of his ministry.

The pastors of the Church must come to grips with this major problem. It is pastorally counterproductive to fail to affirm lay people whose witness, ministry and priesthood is exercised in the dynamics of the workaday world.

2. *What everyone is supposed to be about.* Father David Knight, a popular author and preacher from Memphis, Tennessee, had a tremendous insight several years ago in a booklet he wrote called "Poverty, Who Needs It?" Father Knight said in this booklet that there are basically two kinds of spirituality in the Church—a spirituality of monasticism and one of martyrdom.

His position is that all priests, even though they are not monks, actually are expected by the faithful (at least subconsciously) to live as monks with vows of poverty, chastity and obedience. People in the Church do not make the distinction between religious priests and diocesan priests. A priest is a priest is a priest, and like it or not, Fathers, the people expect you to be poor as well as chaste and obedient. How else explain the widespread false notion that diocesan priests, in this country, have such a small compensation for their services to the Church? Priests are given cars as gifts, "because poor Father has such a small salary." But many priests are far from poor, and I am not speaking about those priests who have become notorious for their wealth. I am speaking about the average pastor in an average middle-class, white, suburban parish.

The priest, in the monastic model of spirituality, is called from the world to minister to the lay people of the Church. It is lay people who are to live in the world. Priests (and religious Brothers and Sisters as well) are not expected to be in public office, to lobby for the poor, to demonstrate in streets.

If anyone does this, it is the lay person.

On the other hand, Father Knight explains, lay people live a spirituality of martyrdom. They risk "death" because, though they must depend on the world for their livelihood, they preach to the world a Gospel it hates. They alienate the world at the risk of losing their jobs, their homes, their social positions.

That's where the martyrdom comes in: a salesman refuses to lie to people buying a used car while his boss has a sales quota hanging over his head and the kids need braces and shoes and he's broke and needs this sale.

If only lay people realized the power of the Gospel and the Spirit that lives in them! If only they would come to the church on Sunday for refreshment, for direction, for a show of strength in their battle for the Lord and for souls in the world! But most do not. They do not see themselves as the Church actively engaged in battle. They are only blessed by the Church (the hierarchy), but they are not the Church.

Even in the best of our churches, lay people are seldomly "sent" into the world as disciples. We do not have, in the Catholic Church, a good understanding of the missionary challenge right under our noses. We minister to people who are working for a living, who have families to feed. Somehow, we want only to heal them, to feed them, to teach them to "have faith in God and he will make all your sufferings bear fruit." We never send them! We never tell them they have the power of God to change things, that the Holy Spirit will give them courage to face their employers and refuse to cheat, to abuse employees, to practice discrimination, to condone drinking and sexual harrassment. We never tell our Catholic people—or other Christians—that they must be militant in their defense of Christian values in society, that they are as free as anyone to influence legislation, that changing the world through political and social structures is as holy a thing as working in a soup kitchen or in a Catholic hospital.

We never tell the people of God that when they fight for the faith, when they assume the responsibility of changing society for the good, that they honor the entire Church, they honor God, they share the martyr's crown.

In recent years, a number of lay people in this nation have been actively preaching the Gospel from pulpits, giving parish missions and retreats. These lay people have brought the spirituality of martyrs into the pulpit, the parish hall.

As the new Code of Canon Law recognizes, it is good that lay people, including women, are encouraged to preach the Gospel—and sometimes even to address the congregation during the liturgy as long as they are not the official homilists.

Lay people can often speak more clearly to lay people than can the clergy.

It comes as a shock to many people, priests included, when they are reminded that Jesus was a layman. He was never ordained. He was a layman. That should make the laity stop to think about the good they can do as lay people.

I think lay people must speak clearly, strongly and courageously about who they are in the Church—but more importantly, about who they are as *Church in the world*.

Perhaps some lay people have become too "churchy" in their effort to define themselves. Parish push to the contrary, it is okay, all right, holy, simply to go to Mass and live out a life of Christian witness in the world.

The primary role of the laity is to be Christ in the world and for the world, to be countercultural when culture is evil or amoral, to be a lover of the poor and oppressed when it is dangerous to do so because power rules rampant.

All Christians should be a part of the community of faith, should be nourished there, should find their strength and direction through parish liturgy as well as personal prayer. Some lay people are called to specific parish ministries, but they are the exception rather than the rule. Theirs is not the ministerial model to hold forth for all lay people.

Lay people must not be two-legged church mice. They must have a say in what happens in the parish, but their influence on parish liturgy and policy must reflect their experience of a missionary life in the world and their outreach to the world.

Catholic lay people must bring the full Gospel to the Chamber of Commerce, town hall and school-board meetings, to the PTA, Full Gospel and civic groups. The Church must promote and teach the truth that lay people perform a priestly act when they live the Gospel in the marketplace, when they build a good cabinet, when they weld a good joint in a steel structure, when they treat patients, or teach children, or walk a beat, or put out fires, or drive a garbage truck, or bag groceries.

If these are not priestly functions for baptized Christians, baptism has lost some of its meaning.

Lay people are the real presence of Jesus as they live the Gospel in favorable and adverse situations. They, as priests of Jesus Christ, offer themselves as he did, as a sacrifice for others.

You see, the most important thing in the Church is to be a baptized Christian. Without baptism, there is no priesthood. The ordained ministry is rooted in the priesthood of the People of God that is passed on to us through baptism. It is in baptism that we first receive the Holy Spirit, with all his gifts. Ordination—like matrimony—gives us a special call in the Church to function, minister, lead and serve in specific ways. But it is baptism that makes it all happen, so to speak.

When people are baptized, they are given, by God, all they need to be effective witnesses in the world. Sometimes, it takes a special event or tragedy to get us on our knees and thinking about who we are as Christians.

The charismatics have rediscovered what scripture calls the "baptism of the Holy Spirit." This is not a sacrament but an experience, sort of an actual grace. Through this experience (read the second and tenth chapters of Acts), God's graces are stirred up in the human heart and a person's mind is opened to see the depth of God's love and power in the faithful disciple. The charismatic gifts are usually manifested when a person receives the baptism of the Holy Spirit, especially the gift of tongues.

However it is done, lay people must be given an opportunity to discover their dignity as Christians, their power as disciples of the Lord, their role as martyrs for the Gospel, their mission in the world and their place in the ministering Church that sends them out to evangelize, to heal, to teach, to preach, to admonish, to encourage, to console.

I will not here quote the documents of Vatican Council II, but I do encourage everyone who has not done so to read the documents on *The Church, The Church in the Modern World,* and *On the Laity.*

Now I must turn to a special group of lay people who are experiencing special needs and problems in the Church at this time. More than half of all lay Catholics in the world have a more difficult time being recognized and employing their talents fully in the service of the Church. I am speaking of women.

Women feel discrimination at all levels—on parish staffs, in chanceries and in official ministries of the Church.

The most controversial issue concerning women in the Church is the question of ordination. Women cannot be deacons or priests by present discipline in the Church. Will that ever change? I don't know. There are many respected theologians who believe that someday it might change. The Holy Father says that it will not change. Many bishops agree with the pope's position.

I am caught in the middle of this dilemma. I have studied under and worked with outstanding Catholic Christians who happened to be women. They love, they serve, they worship, they pray—and they would like the option to become ordained ministers in the Roman Catholic Church. I look at these women and see such potential. I see greater dedication and zeal than among some of the ordained men. I see gifts that could be employed in preaching, in leading liturgies. I see, too, their pain, their frustration.

But the question of justice for women in the Church is more fundamental than the question of ordination. In most cases women are treated as second-class Catholics, people who are required by social custom (even in the Church!) to work for less money even though they are more qualified than their male counterparts, people whose opinions must always be taken with a grain of salt because they are, after all, "only women."

Mother Angelica does not want to be a priest. She agrees with the Holy Father's position. But can anyone deny that if women were someday to be ordained Mother Angelica would be a great candidate for bishop?

Look at what this woman has done because she has had faith and because she is strong. Founding the world's first Catholic TV satellite network in the backyard of a cloistered convent is not the easiest mission imaginable!

I mention Mother Angelica for two reasons. First, she is a woman of great strength and great talent. She is the epitome of what women can do in the Church. Second, she accomplished what she did (what all the U.S. bishops together have not yet been able to do!) without being ordained. She did not need ordination to move millions of people to greater faith through television. She did not need ordination to erect a satellite network. She did not need ordination to marshall the efforts of thousands of lay people around the world to pass out her poor little pamphlets that touched hearts, brought people to conversion, changed people's minds when they had been bent on suicide.

It is not necessary to be ordained to do great things, to exercise fully your ministry in the Church—unless, of course, you are called to the ordained ministry by God.

Sometimes, when I think about the great churchwomen I know, those women who have helped shape my life and ministry, I wonder really if ordination would help them at all.

Oh, I realize that for them it is not simply a question of their not being ordained but the rule against any woman being ordained. They see this as discrimination, as sort of a class distinction, as an injustice against them because they are women.

Part of me, my head, agrees. In pastoral-ministry training, on my way to commissioning as a lay minister, I had to come to grips with my own prejudices against women. It was a painful experience. I had to learn to discuss the question of women priests calmly. The subject used to anger me. It angered me because it threatened me. I realized finally that part of my identity as a *man* was that I was *over* women. Now that has to be a little sick! Just as sick as white people needing subservient blacks to make them (the whites) feel important.

Still, in my heart, I cannot "see" women priests. Perhaps it is still an emotional thing. Perhaps it is divine wisdom. Perhaps it is still prejudice. All I know is that when I think about man and woman, I see the warrior and the mother, the breadearner and the homemaker. I see equally important, but different, roles for men and women.

I am convinced that mothers should be at home with their children. I believe families should live in smaller homes, drive older cars, buy less-expensive clothing, never eat out and take fewer vacations if that's what it takes to keep mothers at home with their little children. I hate the fact that the state takes our children away from us at such an early age. There was the first grade, then kindergarten, then pre-kindergarten. Now there are nursery schools and day-care centers. We are losing our children to the state—and all in the name of a "better" way of life.

The greatest gift a couple can make to the world is a family of well-loved and well-disciplined children.

I believe a mother in the home is crucial to the development of children. I don't think a father, usually, can do the job as well. I don't think a career as a doctor is more important to society than a vocation as a mother. Sorry. I just don't believe it.

I realize that women must be free to make the choices best for them. I realize that many women will disagree strongly with my position—but that is my position. I want to grow, to understand. I would hope that those who disagree with me or with the official position of the Church are also willing to grow, to understand. I hope they, like me, realize that their opinion is not necessarily the correct one, even if it seems to be the most innovative or courageous.

Happily, women minister without ordination. They've been doing it for years.

Perhaps the first thing we need to do is to realize that they are first-class Christians, to treat them with respect and dignity, to judge their work by the same standards we use for judging the work of men, by giving them the same breaks in lay leadership positions in the Church.

I know that some parishes around the nation have religious Sisters serving as administrators. Some have deacons. Some have lay people, even married couples, serving together as leaders of parishes when no priests are available.

I believe we are well into a new era, the true age of the laity, brought on, not by vision or inspiration, but necessity. I believe we are going to realize that, regardless of the outcome of arguments about women and/or married priests, that the job of pastor can be filled by someone other than an ordained priest. I can see parishes pastored by lay people, deacons and religious Sisters and Brothers and "circuit priests" who will celebrate Eucharist as often as they can.

This is indeed happening in Third World countries and even here in our own country.

Lay people have the grace and the right to minister in the Church and no one—pope, bishop or priest—can take that right away from them unless they abuse it.

It is said that the Church is not a democracy. I agree—but I can't help but realize that for several years now the laity have indeed been voting in the Church—with their feet. They have left the Church when they have felt abandoned, unloved, unrecognized, unimportant. It will take ministering lay people to get those people back into the ministering community.

One of the most powerful movements in the Church today is the RENEW process of spiritual growth. This process calls people into small groups to share their faith, their hopes, dreams, problems.

I am convinced the future of the Church lies in the small Christian communities that grow in faith through home meetings and then come together on Sunday in the parish Church to celebrate their faith. These communities can be the strength of the Church of the next century or they can be a terrible source of division. But, either way, we will have small communities.

If leaders in the Church can make Christian communities a priority, as does the RENEW process, we will have *Catholic* Christian communities forming in neighborhoods around the nation. These communities will look to the parish for overall direction, for unifying force of Eucharist and Word.

But if Church leadership continues to go on with "business as usual" and fails to meet the communitarian needs of people, by embracing these small communities and changing ministerial patterns to accommodate them, then we will lose many of these people to revolution, to fundamentalism or to secularism.

It is a challenge we cannot ignore. It is not a question of giving lay people power, but of recognizing the power of God in them and his call to them to come together in meaningful relationships.

Lay people must unite, under the guidance of their bishops and pastors, into small Eucharist-centered groups whose faith leads them to bear witness, as willing martyrs, to a Gospel the world hates.

Chapter 8

A WORD ABOUT BISHOPS, PRIESTS AND DEACONS

I realize that most people reading this book are lay people, but there are several issues that involve priests and bishops in which they, too, often feel caught in the middle.

For example, when certain priests lose their identity and question their vocations, other priests, even bishops also experience pain and conflict. The trauma of one priest affects his brother priests and his bishop as well as the laity.

In fact, lay people must realize they frequently, though mostly inadvertently, contribute to the distress affecting many priests today. While priests and bishops often feel they are ultimately responsible for what happens in the Church, they must realize they are not God. Lay people have to be responsible for themselves. They are Christians—and they have responsibilities to God, to one another and to their pastors.

I think many problems in the Church today are rooted in how clergy view and treat laity and vice versa. Let's take a look at clergy-lay relationships.

A good friend of mine, Lida Gall from Crowley, Louisiana, once said, "Poor God! When things go wrong, he gets the blame. If we are sick, it's God's will. If someone dies, it's God's will. If someone loses a job, it's God's will. But if we're well, or don't die or don't lose our job, it's 'What great luck!'"

I think bishops and priests have the same problem. A few significant examples come to mind.

In the summer of 1986 when it came to light that a number of aged nuns were suffering severe poverty, everyone was quick to blame the bishops. The bishops were responsible for taking care of the nuns, it was said, and that is true. However, whatever lay people want, lay people get. If they want to build a new football stadium for one thousand students in the local Catholic school, or when they want to build a new soccer field, a new church or a new softball diamond, lay people somehow get the funds and the approval of bishops and pastors. If lay people were really concerned about the nuns (and about lay employees working in the Church) funds would be available for just treatment of these people.

In their 1986 pastoral message, popularly known as "Economic Justice for All," the U.S. bishops alluded to the fact that lay people themselves do not have a great desire for justice. The bishops admitted their own responsibility to lay people, priests and religious working full-time for the Church. But they said, too, that these "obligations cannot be met without the increased contributions of all the members of the church" (no. 351).

In 1985-86, when several priests were accused of and admitted sexually molesting children, everyone pointed fingers at the bishops. Why didn't *the bishops* foresee all this? Why did they handle it so badly when the crime was discovered? Why did they remain silent when they should have spoken to the issue?

But everyone in the Church shares the burden—including priests who should have been brothers to these sick men whose frustration, anger, fear and loneliness found expression in sexual perversion. Lay people must share responsibility for their priests— for those who sin so terribly as well as for those whose sins are not considered so terrible.

It is lay people who put priests (and other pastoral leaders) on pedestals and isolate them from intimacy - or lay people permit their priests to impose this exile upon themselves.

Some priests think I am an anticlerical. I am not. Goodness! I *am* a cleric myself! But for years, as a layman, I mounted a one-man attack on pedestals. I loved toppling them over. Sadly, I did not often think to catch the man who was falling from the pedestal. I thought, in those days, that he always climbed up there himself. I didn't realize how many Catholics push and shove until their priest is safely up above them, like God, unreachable and unable to reach them!

I want to topple pedestals, but I don't want people to fall to the ground. I want the community to catch them as they fall, or to persuade them to come down before they fall. But in any case the pedestals must come down.

We must learn to express love for our priests in new ways, not in isolation and apartness—but not in ways that would test their mettle as celibates either. I have seen too many women drape themselves over priests, as though this were a sign of real Christian love. They are fooling no one, not even themselves. Perhaps their husbands do not show them enough affection. Perhaps they have suffered rejection. Perhaps they have unhealthy desires and unwholesome designs. Whatever, such conduct can make good priests "gun shy" and limit their ability to show affection to others.

It is essential that priests show affection to everyone, including women. It is essential that priests can let themselves be loved by both men and women.

When I see priests draw away from normal expressions of affection or hold themselves apart from their communities, I want to say to them, "Fathers, I want you to know that you can let yourselves be loved without endangering your vow of celibacy. You can be loved and loved abundantly by the community, by individuals in community, even by women in the community, without sinning, without endangering your vows. We married men have to learn to do that, to hug the sisters in the community without going into a clinch, to kiss with love but not with passion.

"You must seek genuine, human and chaste love. You must cope constructively with the advances of people seeking to weaken you, but you must find ways in which to love and be loved intimately."

Some of our greatest saints had prayer-partners of the opposite sex. Actually, if a priest or bishop does have a strong, holy Catholic woman with whom he is in a prayerful relationship, his ministry will be all the richer, more human, more loving.

I am terribly concerned about young priests coming out of seminaries these days. They are told to be celibate in a very earthy world. They are lonely and unsure of themselves. After all, they are still, for the most part, young adults themselves who for several years have been set apart from the general community. I think they cover up their insecurity with a certain unhealthy brashness. It's sometimes called a "negative sense of humor," the kind of cutting humor that insults. It's Archie Bunker humor. But here we are not involved in a sitcom; we're talking about real life, parish life, relationships with flesh and blood people. This brashness is not healthy —and I think it comes from a lack of intimacy, a lack of home and family life. From what I hear, the average rectory in this country provides little in terms of fraternal community and wholesome intimacy.

Bishops and priests need love and intimacy, but they must shun adulation. Adulation is superfluous praise, a special kind of pedestal.

Again, I say to priests, "People who give you such empty praise are holding you at arms length, and as their pastor, you must challenge this emptiness. You must be loving and charitable, but you must force these people to love you humanly, fully and as a man. You must call them into relationship with yourself, because as they treat you, so they treat God. If they fear a relationship with one of God's ministers, they probably fear a relationship with God.

"You do not need adulation. You need the kind of love that will grieve with you when your mother dies, the kind of love that will console you and assure you of God's forgiveness when you have sinned, the kind of love that will build you up by sharing your failures as well as your successes, the kind of love that lets you be fully human, completely broken, completely vulnerable and completely in need of the same salvation your congregation so badly needs.

And if I could speak to all lay people in the Church, I'd tell them, "You don't need to put your priest on a pedestal to protect his power to absolve and consecrate. He is a sinner. Everytime he lifts his hand in absolution, every time he elevates the consecrated host, it is the hand of a sinner that absolves, the hand of a sinner that holds God himself aloft for worship. The priest must be our brother in faith before he can be our father in faith."

Baptism is the source of our common faith, the source of all degrees, levels and expressions of the priesthood of Jesus. If priests and bishops, and yes, even the pope, are not first our brothers in the Lord, if they do not share the same need of salvation, if they are not baptized with the same water, then they can never be our Fathers in faith.

I believe in the priesthood. I revere the priesthood. I love priests as individual human beings. I do not lump them all into one big blob called "priest." I see them as individual Christians, struggling with their own spiritual life, sometimes especially aware of their unworthiness to proclaim the Gospel, to hold up the consecrated host, to raise their hands in absolution. But they are men of great courage, great humility, for they do not stop ministering. They do not run away. Instead, they swallow bitter pride and guilt and shame, doing so to honor God and to serve God's people, in ministry, in the ministry only they can perform, ministry which they, themselves, as broken Christians, seek out for healing.

How dare we load burdens on their shoulders by not letting them be human? How dare we set them up as whipping boys whom we blame if we do not live up to our obligations as Christians. We say it is their fault that we are angry, hurt or turned off. They offended us. What a lie! We all have free will. We choose our responses. We make the decision to stop going to Mass, to stop giving in the collection.

Sure. Some priests are hypocrites. But as one prison chaplain said, "If a hypocrite is standing between you and God, the hypocrite is closer to God than you are!"

If a priest is in error, he needs love, prayers and encouragement, not condemnation or self-righteous indignation.

I truly love the priesthood. It fascinates me. I am fascinated when I watch a priest's hands during Mass—the hands, once anointed with chrism, destined for all time to bless, to absolve. I am fascinated with those hands that call the Holy Spirit down upon the bread and wine, that hold up the Lord of lords and the King of kings for the congregation to worship.

What a tremendous gift is the consecrated voice of a priest, a voice that calls people to repentance, to worship, to service, to community, a voice that blesses, that speaks the good news of forgiveness. And a voice that speaks the ancient words that change bread and wine into the body and blood of Jesus.

How fascinated I am with the priesthood! And yet, as I look upon these men, good and sometimes not so good, I see men struggling with their own humanity, their own need for forgiveness.

Their weakness, their humanness strangely does not weaken their ministry. Their humanness does not taint their worship nor limit their power to consecrate and absolve. Rather, because priests are only ordained sinners, the wonder and beauty of priesthood increases. Because God uses sinful men for his most sacred of ministries on earth, we can all be sure that God uses us and lives in us and loves us as we fight for spiritual victory against our own sins and the sins of a secular, amoral and sinful world.

The priesthood, with its sinful men, is one of God's most precious gifts to his Church of sinful people. Jesus himself, St. Paul says, *became sin* to save us. Is it any surprise or cause for scandal that he now comes in and through sinners to proclaim that magnificent mystery?

In our own St. Mary Magdalen Parish there is tremendous respect for the priests. But more than in any other parish I know, the priests are loved as human beings, not as religious functionaries. They are called Father—but they call others "sister" and "brother." They cement faith-relationships with shared brokenness, shared hope, shared sorrow, shared joy.

In our parish, there is widespread lay ministry, constant affirmation of all ministers, ongoing education and formation for all ministers. There are staff meetings and staff retreats, lay ministry updates, large community gatherings for celebration of major parish milestones and anniversaries, penance services that fill the church to overflowing.

The priests, deacons, religious and lay ministers of the parish call forth the gifts from the community—with 300 lay ministers to the sick and scores of others in ministry to the divorced and remarried, to young adults and youth, to the elderly, to the unemployed and the poor.

There is no time for identity crises. The priests' affirmation comes from the dynamics of shared ministry, from the people of the parish, our own bishop and their brother priests.

But not all parishes are as blessed with clergy and laity as is our parish. In fact, there are parishes in which the pastor is suffering from ministerial burnout or some sort of serious distress. There are pastors who are unnerved by lay people who want to minister and unnerved even more by the presence of a permanent deacon. Some priests are suffering tremendous spiritual problems. In such parishes, the Church suffers together but somehow never quite comes together.

I hear serious criticism from Catholics throughout the U.S. that bears repeating here. While Catholics generally love their priests and want to support them, they feel abandoned by their bishops when "bad" priests are not effectively relieved of ministry and put in either medical or spiritual programs designed to bring about healing and/or repentance.

Sometimes charity means doing what is hardest to do—call a man to task, permit a parish to be priestless for a while to protect the standard of ministry, the faith of the people.

Now on to another complaint, namely, the failure of the Church to practice what it preaches when it comes to justice in the Church. I speak here of the total Church, including laity along with bishops and priests.

I am very much aware of the U.S. bishops' courageous pastorals on war and peace and on the economy. I am aware of their praiseworthy interest in bettering the lot of women in both society and the Church—and of their gigantic strides toward helping the poor break the "hellish cycle of poverty." The bishops also have shown genuine leadership in trying to make lay people a more effective part of the Church's mission.

There are many volunteer lay people working in effective ministries in the Church. Their number should grow.

With the growing interest in religion in this country, however, the Church will need more full-time lay ministers and employees to keep up with the needs of the community and to develop a more extensive and effective evangelistic outreach.

I realize that bishops and priests feel caught in the middle of great demands on the Church's financial and human resources, and the widely proclaimed absence of adequate personnel and funds to meet the demands. Needs grow faster than resources.

But finally we get down to the question of values and priorities that uphold our values or make them out to be a lie. If lay Church employees throughout the country are telling the truth, the Church is not paying fair wages. Here the bishops are very directly involved in a question of justice. They are aware of the needs of families. They say so in their sermons and in their pastorals. They argue that employers, including the Church itself, must pay fair wages and enhance family life through proper working conditions and benefits.

The bishops have long been vocal in support of the right of employees to organize and they speak out again in "Economic Justice for All." They say, too, that even Church employees have the right to organize (no. 353).

I know some Catholic newspapers have associations of employees; some others, the newspaper guild. I am convinced that if the Church had practiced justice from the outset, these organizations would not have been necessary.

I think it is a gross insult to Jesus and his Gospel that Church employees need, or feel they need, to organize for justice. Instead of guilds, associations and unions, we are supposed to be about Christian community and ministry and mission!

Be that as it may, a growing number of lay people, who do not work for the Church, are saying as forcefully as they can: "We will believe the bishops are serious about justice when they begin to practice justice themselves." I pray now, that after speaking so clearly in their 1986 pastoral, the bishops will make justice a priority in their own organizations. I hasten to emphasize, however, that employees have a responsibility to justice as well.

Perhaps the U.S. bishops could solve the "justice problem in the Church" by courageous and innovative action. I offer one suggestion as a possible step in the right direction. Perhaps the bishops in the U.S. could initiate a nationwide reconciliation process between Church "managers" and Church "employees" and work toward the concept of team ministry, shared responsibility and justice in love for all.

Again, the bishops alone are not to blame any injustices in the Church. Lay people do not place enough value on lay ministry. There is a mistaken notion, among clergy and laity alike, that a lay employee's dedication can be measured by how underpaid she or he is.

I'll never forget how I felt when a well-to-do lay person told me that I should be willing to work for less because of the honor of serving the Church.

You can't eat honor. Honor doesn't buy shoes or put braces on teeth. Doctors don't give a darn about your honor when you go in for their services. The supermarket prefers cash to character.

People sometimes compare priests' "salaries" with those of lay workers in the Church: "Father works long hours six or seven days a week and he only gets $400 a month. But lay people have a forty-hour work week and make upwards of twelve hundred dollars a month. And don't forget, Father has a *vocation*, so he is a special person."

Priests do work hard (most of them) for small salaries. But there are other considerations besides cash salary.

A priest is provided with all meals, medical insurance, retirement, housing, utilities and automobile. He has a housekeeper and yardman. He usually doesn't do his own laundry, dishes, cooking or lawn. He doesn't usually have to repair plumbing or pay a plumber out of his own pocket. Since he doesn't have a wife and family, if he wants to he can go out to dinner or a movie for the price of one - not two or three or more.

For lay people, work is also part and parcel of *vocation*. Lay people cannot separate their work from their Christian vocation, either in the Church or in the world, any more than a priest can separate his ministry from his vocation.

Lay people who are employed in the Church (or in the world) put in from forty to sixty hours a week on the job. Then they have to go home to cook, do laundry, clean house, iron clothes, mow lawns, paint walls, repair cars, attend school meetings, nurse sick family members, spend time with children and grandchildren—all these things, along with their jobs, are part and parcel of *their* Christian *vocation*. Lay people do not, as priests do not, simply leave work and go home to rest and recreate. Moreover, lay people who work for the Church usually do a lot of volunteer work on the parish and diocesan level as well.

While priests and Sisters give up conjugal love and the joys of family life, they also give up the pain, frustration, fatigue and strain of family life. Celibates can get privacy. Family people cannot. Lay people, in a special way those who are married, are as much "living for others" as are priests and religious.

The question of justice for people employed by the Church, however, is broader than the question of salaries and fringe benefits. It is rooted in the role models and relationships in our Christian communities.

There are two juxtaposed "isms" in the Church causing discord, namely, clericalism and laicism. Clericalism is that malaise that places clergy in a privileged position in the Church, above accountability and beyond intimacy. Laicism is that disease, born of greed for power and spiritual ignorance, which leads laity to seek control of the Church so they can run it their way.

A move toward justice in the Church, I believe, would be to bury forever the "class" distinction (clergy versus laity) that gives rise to separatism, confrontation, abuse, dissension.

We need to move toward being daughters and sons of the same Father, sisters and brothers all, before we can begin to pastor, to minister and to serve as equals and coheirs of the Kingdom.

Until we clean up our own house, we can hardly be taken seriously by those outside our communion, those who have no faith in Jesus.

The bishops and many religious educators today are speaking about justice as being part of evangelization. If that is so, injustices in the Church will kill any message of faith we are trying to preach.

I will talk about evangelization in the last chapter of this book. But while I am emphasizing the importance of lay ministry and of justice for lay people (and religious) in the Church, it cannot be emphasized too strongly that the clergy, with all their high profile, have a tremendous impact on evangelization.

It is so easy to criticize, to find fault, to chastise and urge priests on to reform.

If lay people truly loved their priests, helped them set priorities, supported them in their own struggles toward holiness, the clergy would be far more effective.

We would have fewer priests working themselves to death simply to prove they have value. They would see, through our love, that they have innate value. We could help our Fathers in faith discover they have value in our eyes and the eyes of God—in all their brokenness and aside from all ministry. There are people, priests included, who feel that to be of any value at all, they have to keep busy and achieve constantly. This refutes alleged faith in the Gospel that tells us we are so valuable in God's eyes that we are worth the passion and death of Jesus. At our worst moment, in our deepest sin (child abuse, alcoholism, injustice, racial bigotry, whatever), in the eyes of the Father we were worth Jesus' death.

Lay people want and need solid spiritual leadership from their priests. That doesn't mean priests are sinless. It means priests are praying, repenting, working hard and playing hard, eating a good diet, getting enough sleep, taking sufficient exercise, relating to all the other sinners in the parish.

Lay people want priests whose faith makes their sermons credible, whose preaching reflects personal belief and hope in Jesus, whose teaching reflects the teachings of the universal Church, respects the magisterium, explains the mysteries of faith as well as possible, encourages people to pursue holiness and excites them enough to share their faith.

The community of faith needs priests who truly worship at liturgy, whose celibate life style speaks of the immanence of God as well as his transcendence, whose devotion to the Word and the Eucharist reminds people of the dynamic power of their God and his willingness to intervene in everyday situations to bless, heal and deliver his people.

I am utterly convinced that celibacy is a tremendous gift for the Church. I am equally convinced that if ever the Church and the world needed that gift, it is now. Celibacy speaks clearly of devotion to God and Church because it is so dramatic a grace, so demanding a choice. It is demanding but not more so than marriage. It is merely demanding in a different way. As convinced as I am that the Church needs a celibate witness today, I realize that the witness of celibacy alone is not enough for the proclamation of the Gospel. The witness of both celibacy and sacramental conjugality must go hand-in-hand to proclaim the Gospel if the Gospel is to be proclaimed in fullness.

I've already talked about marriage as a model for the Church in any given parish and also about Father Knight's monastic and martyr models of spirituality.

While both conjugal spirituality and celibate spirituality bear full witness to the gospel, each emphasizes different but special aspects of faith and spirituality.

Celibacy is a gift that reminds us of the future Kingdom, the second coming, the transcendence of the God who, surprisingly, lives within us. Sacramental conjugality is a community of faith, a sign of the Kingdom already here—but not yet. Conjugality speaks of an immanent God without denying his transcendence.

Both celibacy and conjugality are such precious gifts. Both are gifts of sexuality. In marriage, a man and woman use their sexual energy to express the intimate love of God for each person, they procreate life, they proclaim the creative power of God. Their exclusive love underscores the intensity of God's love for each individual. In their conjugality, as they live and love, offend and forgive, they remind the Church of the redemptive love of Jesus.

The celibate, who is single for the sake of the Kingdom, redirects energy into an agape love for all people. The male or female celibate images God's love for his entire people. The celibate is more obviously "for all the people." How else explain the confidence people have in the celibate priest compared with the married lay leader? There is something prophetic in the celibate that is not as obvious in the married person. The celibate's human embrace is for all; her or his spiritual embrace encompasses all—as a priority, not as a second thought or a second vocation. The celibate, who is celibate for the sake of the Kingdom, is the husband, wife, servant of all.

The celibate's spiritual embrace calls everyone out of themselves into the Father, Son, Spirit. They point to the Kingdom that can be, to that spiritual dimension that flesh alone cannot see.

Both celibates and married people point to the Kingdom. They do so in different ways. Each witness is necessary. Only through both witnesses, side-by-side and complementing each other, can the fullness of Gospel and Church be realized.

In our parish, we have one of the first married Catholic priests in the U.S. He was formerly an Anglican priest, but along with others, with the approval of Rome, has become a Catholic priest who remains actively married. His ministry in the parish is very successful. Father Larry Lossing preaches well. He is a good counselor. He is sought out by people of all ages, both married and single. He is fully a priest. He absolves from sin. He consecrates the Eucharist. He presides at liturgies.

He is not, however, a celibate. His witness is fully priestly, but not a celibate witness. He is both a ministering priest and conjugal lover. The other parish priests are celibate lovers. We are most fortunate, in our parish, to have such a combination of priesthood, celibate and conjugal. Somehow it places the whole concept of priesthood, celibate and conjugal, in a new perspective—and creates as well a new dynamic.

Add to this combination the active ministry of myself and two other permanent deacons, all very well married, and St. Mary Magdalen Parish becomes a real testing ground for different expressions and styles of ordained ministry. The whole experience is delightfully exciting and rewarding.

Of course, in accepting ordination to the diaconate, I agreed that if Peg should die before I do I would remain celibate. The same holds true for Father Lossing and the other two permanent deacons. My struggle with the possibility of future celibacy, with seeking ordination and the impact of these deliberations on my marital relationship, speak to the entire issue of priesthood, ordained ministry and celibacy.

Deciding to be a deacon was a tough decision. I was being pulled two ways. I've always been proud of being a lay person. I've believed that my dedication to the Church as a lay person had perhaps more meaning to some people than the dedication of a priest or nun.

At the same time, I felt a tug toward the ordained ministry. I saw ordination as an empowerment to preach, to minister. I wanted to preach more effectively. From the earliest days of Vatican Council II, when the idea of restoration of the ancient order of deacon was raised, I wanted to be a deacon.

In the Orlando diocese, men seeking ordination to the diaconate must first complete three years of intensive study, reflection and training as lay pastoral ministers. After being commissioned as a lay pastoral minister, those men who want to pursue the diaconate must apply for training and undergo additional psychological testing.

As I entered the third year of training as a lay pastoral minister, Peg and I were, along with several other couples, thinking about applying for the fourth year of training toward possible ordination in the diaconate.

In those third-year reflections, my concerns were capsuled in three basic questions.

1. *Am I more effective for God and Church as a layman or would I be more effective as a deacon?* For years, I had ministered effectively as a lay person. And I cherished this role. I was one of the few lay people in the nation who was actively preaching from Catholic pulpits during weekend Masses.

The permission to preach at homily time was originally granted to permit me to promote *The Florida Catholic*. Later, after Sister Briege prayed with me, priests began to ask me to preach more on the scriptures and to "only mention the paper as you go along." This resulted in two things. First, I found I was gifted as a preacher and that people responded favorably to my preaching. Second, because I was preaching a spiritual message based on the Sunday readings, more people than ever picked up the available copies of the paper. We learned a valuable lesson—don't prostitute the pulpit. Preach the Gospel, and if you do it right, people will want to read your paper.

2. *Is God calling me or am I calling myself?* It is easy to convince yourself God is calling you even if he isn't. Good will, the desire to serve, the "glamor" of the ministry—all can be mistaken as a call from the Lord and his Church. It takes prayer and discernment—a lot of both—to determine a real call.

3. *If I say yes to the diaconate, which means celibacy if Peg dies before I do, what does this say to Peg?* Is it telling her my life with her is not so important after all?

After much prayer and consultation and sharing with Peg and other friends, I decided that I was already a churchman—after twenty-seven years of full-time work in the Church—and being a deacon would not limit my witness. Once that question had been answered, it was easy to believe that God was calling me. Too many people were affirming the call, including Peg, our children, my pastor, the parish staff, Father David Page (my boss at *The Florida Catholic*), several deacon-friends, and my little prayer community.

The final question, about celibacy, was not easy to resolve. Peg and I had talked about the celibacy issue with Father David Ferguson, director of our diaconate program in the Orlando diocese.

I told Father Dave and Peg that I didn't think I would ever want to remarry. I didn't and still don't think I could give myself as fully to another woman as I have to Peg, and marriage requires total giving. I still had not, however, been able to identify the cause of my concern about Peg's possible reaction to my decision to chance ultimate celibacy. Later, after much more prayer and reflection, while writing in my journal, the matter about Peg's feelings became clear—and I could at last name what was gnawing away inside.

I was worried that Peg would feel offended if I could chose celibacy over married life—even as a remote possibility. Would she see this as a hidden desire to be a priest and not be married? Would she feel second best? Finally, in our last serious discussion about applying for the fourth year of training with hopes for ordination, I told her about my concern.

She immediately said she had no misgivings or reservations, that the celibacy requirement caused her no concern.

We applied.

We were accepted.

The fourth year of formation in our diocese was billed as "a time of reflection and discernment." I still had to struggle with the notion of God calling me. While I felt sure I had a call to the diaconate, I knew I needed to pray more, to continue to discern, to achieve some degree of detachment so that I could really surrender myself to God's will.

Could I pray, "Thy will be done," or did that prayer frighten me? I wanted to be a deacon, but I wanted to do God's will. But if God didn't want me to be a deacon, which did I want more—the diaconate or God's will?

That is, as an evangelical preacher said, "where the rubber meets the road."

About the middle of our fourth year of training, Father Dave

asked us to do a paper on "Why I Want to Be a Deacon." I wrote
the paper on a visit back home, in Henry, Louisiana. I had Dad
drop me off at the old parish church. I sat there, in the first pew,
looking at the sanctuary where I had served for more than fifteen
years as altar boy. I looked at the pulpit, remembering the sermons
I had heard. I could still hear the voice of the Dutch pastor, Father
Verheem, as he preached. Even today, as I mentioned earlier,
when I have tough decisions to make, his voice echoes from the
past, "Do good. Trust God. Pray and he will help you."

I knelt and prayed to the Lord present in the tabernacle.

Why, indeed, did I want to become a deacon? I reflected again
on my three questions and answers. I thought of the encouragement from so many people—but encouragement and affirmation
are not necessarily the sign of a call.

"Why, Lord, do I want to be a deacon?" Slowly, the answer
came. As it unfolded, I wrote my paper. It took the form of a letter
to Father Dave. I want to share much of that letter with you. I think
it speaks of vocation, priesthood, service.

"As I sit in my old parish church, I am so conscious of the passing
of my youth, of so much wasted time; yet, I am conscious, too,
that because of both the pleasant and unpleasant, of the good
times and the bad, the good works and the failures, I am who and
what I am ... Here I felt called to the altar, and had 'visions' of being a missionary to darkest Africa.

"I realize so clearly this morning that Father Verheem (even re-
calling his impatient frustration with us dumb country bumpkins)
had much to do with my vocation to marriage, my avocation to the
Catholic press, my call to ministry and, may it please God, my
vocation to the diaconate.

"I want to be an ordained deacon. I guess I've always wanted
that—ever since I heard of the permanent diaconate.

"The difference today is this. The diaconate, if I am ordained, is
not something that I first reached for or sought out. It is something
to which I was called, an internal prompting, a residual inspiration
that has moved me ever closer to the Lord in faith, love and service. And the first recollections of that inner prompting are here at
St. John's. The call has been echoed and amplified in my Catholic

press ministry, in my faith experiences and ministry at St. Mary Magdalen Parish and in the Orlando diocese.

"To paraphrase the Word, how can I reach for something I've never seen; how could I see it if it was not revealed? The call is from the Lord or I would not know it since above all I seek his will (well, sometimes!) ...

"At prayer early this morning an old song came to mind - 'Love and marriage, love and marriage, they go together like a horse and carriage.' This song came out of 'nowhere' as I was reflecting on 'Why *do* I want to be a deacon?' The song said to me, if a man and woman love, they are called to a sacramental relationship. If a man and woman are in a sacramental relationship, they are in love.

"I guess I hear the call to diaconate so clearly because I hear the call to marriage so clearly, because my relationship with Peg is so good and free and strong and right, because she hears the call with me, because I am already intimate with vocation.

"I do love the Lord. I do love the Church. Peg and I together have already laid down our lives for the Church. It is only 'natural' for me that my love for the Church would evolve in a deeper sacramental relationship growing from baptism, nourished in Eucharist. I consider my deepening and particular relationship with the Lord and his Church so real and tangible that both the Church and I need to touch it, hold it, bless it, embrace it, love it, name it, ritualize and sacramentalize it.

"To me, that means ordination.

"I am very much aware of my brokenness, my sinfulness. Part of me is the ham, the actor, the up-front, high profile (sometimes arrogant) public figure. That's not *all* bad. I'm built that way. Basically, it is a gift. I'm working hard to subdue self and let the Lord use me as he will.

"On the positive side of brokenness, I can tell others struggling with pride, lust, gluttony and chemical abuse: 'I have been there, let's walk a ways together.'

"I no longer see leadership (or even evangelization) as something someone does *for* or *to* others. Christian leadership is first of all becoming one-with-others or it is neither Christian nor leadership.

"I see my diaconal altar service as representative of my basic ministry to young adults, in the press and as evangelist. There is some other element I can't quite define, but it has to do with helping to reflect and celebrate all the other ministries and faith-stories in the parish as I serve at the altar.

"If ordained, I think I will be able to bring to the liturgy something very special. At baptisms of infants, I will recall the feelings, joy, pride, and apprehensions I experienced both as parent and god-parent.

"At marriages, I will be able to understand the passion, fear, nervousness and dreams of bride and groom.

"At wakes and funerals, I can empathize with the bereaved and help them celebrate their faith—or perhaps, in some cases, discover faith.

"In visiting the sick, in comforting parents of sick children, I will be able to share personally the terrible agony of watching loved ones suffer and die.

"Peg will be able to help these people also. I hope she will feel free to share these special moments. She is so loving and affirming, and I believe she could do wonders at baptisms, wakes and marriages—by being there and helping people feel at home and loved. If ordained, I surely am going to ask her to share my diaconal service in this way."

Since ordination on Pentecost Sunday, May 18, 1986, I have had many opportunities to preach. I even went back home, to Henry, Louisiana, at St. John the Evangelist Parish. I preached in my home parish, where I had first felt the call of God to ordained ministry. It was a magnificent experience. And I preached at Our Lady of Fatima, Lafayette, where my first editor, Msgr. Alexander O. Sigur, is pastor. Two other deacons, long-time friends Jim Oliver and Stan Gall, were present in the sanctuary. What a blessed homecoming that weekend was!

As I stood in the pulpit of my home parish, I remembered all the priests who had served there as pastor, especially Father Verheem and Father Leon Perras who was on loan to the Lafayette diocese from the Archdiocese of Boston. I remembered, too, one other priest, whose sermons touched people deeply, who was always reaching out to people in pain, who visited the sick and brought them the Lord in Communion. This priest I remembered with great sadness. He was the priest who often sat with my Dad and other relatives as Mama underwent cancer surgery—and he was the priest convicted of sexually abusing children.

It was a day of mixed emotions, that day I preached in St. John's pulpit. The new pastor, Father Joe Stemmen, is a great priest, a good man, a man looking to serve, to support the healing process the Lord has begun in the parish.

In addition to the honor of preaching among my own people, the people who nurtured my faith, the people whose faith sent me abroad into Church work, it was very thrilling to receive their love and affirmation. After Mass, they came up to me, one after another, shaking my hand, hugging me. There were the parents of kids I grew up with, now bowed with age; there were the kids I grew up with, now grandparents themselves; there was Louise Primeaux, a beloved teacher, beaming with joy. There were Bob and Ruth Broussard and Paul and Louise Libersat, cousins who cared for my dying mother—and Ida and John Mergist who have sort of adopted my ninety-one-year old Dad.

Several people said to me after Mass, with a note of genuine pride, "It's great to see one of our own up there on the altar." I am the first ordinand from the parish.

I had prayed, long and hard, "Dear Lord, use me to bring healing to the parish." Perhaps this simple Cajun pride in "one of our own" will be a healing balm in the aftermath of the scandal in the parish.

I still respect the priest whose sin was so terrible, who brought shame upon himself and lawsuits on his bishop, who now is under a twenty-year sentence at hard labor. I remember with gratitude his ministry to my aging and ailing parents, and with sorrow and sympathy—for him and all families affected—I remember in prayer the sickness, the sin, the heartbreak and pain.

So when I speak to the Fathers of the Church in this book about brokenness, I want them to know that nothing they have ever done is beyond God's mercy and forgiveness. Nothing is beyond the hope of reconciliation with the community of the Church.

As I reflect on the extent of sin in the Church, of the scandals that have prevailed in recent years, I am convinced that the Church in the U.S. is under satanic attack. Yes, Satan is afraid of the revival of faith he sees among God's people. He attacks the family of the Church through the pastors; he attacks the domestic family through the relationships between husbands and wives—and most viciously through children who find themselves drowning in a culture that thrives on violence, drugs and sexual perversion.

I respectfully request that our bishops—no, I beg them—reinstate widespread adoration of the Blessed Sacrament to offset this attack by the enemy. I am convinced that only through eucharistic worship can Catholics recapture the power of their faith, the strength to resist Satan.

Finally, in speaking of the relationships between clergy and laity, we must recognize a shared responsibility in spreading our holy Catholic faith.

I asked Father Tobin, when I was beginning to think about this book, what he thought was the most important spiritual issue facing the Church today. He responded quickly, "Henry, write about baptism and help lay people see the power that they have to change the world and to lead people to Jesus."

He is right. I believe most lay people don't fully appreciate their baptism. They see it as something that took away original sin, whatever that means to them, and made them members of the Church. To be baptized is to be made different, to be someone for the Lord, to have a mission, a place in Church, rights as children of God and Church.

Pope John XXIII once said that the most important day of his life was not the day he was made pope, nor the day he was ordained priest, but the day he was baptized. On that day, he became a Christian, and the fullness of God's call for Angelo Roncalli, to priesthood, episcopacy and papacy, was in that call of baptism.

The call to diaconate, to marriage, to religious life or the priesthood is present in the call of baptism or it is not present at all. Baptism is the basic sacrament, the primal sacrament, the foundation for everything else that goes on in the Church.

We must find a way—through preaching, teaching, or ministries of service—to inspire apathetic Catholics and to call to conversion people who do not know the Lord at all. Otherwise this generation and the next may well be lost to the Church, if indeed, the Lord stays his second coming that long!

Lay people are the evangelizing Church. As Father Knight pointed out so well, pastors and lay ministers are serving the Body of the Lord. It is the fatihful, the People of God who live in the marketplace, who most effectively preach the Gospel in the world.

In the next chapter, the concluding pages of this book, I want to talk to Catholics and other Christians who are too timid or threatened, caught in the middle, so to speak, when they realize they are called to preach and teach the Gospel.

Chapter 9

FROM THE ROOFTOPS

It was during Holy Week, according to John's Gospel. Jesus had just entered Jerusalem. Several Greek Jews had come to worship in Jerusalem. They had seen Jesus enter the city. They most probably had heard a lot about this man, this miracle-worker, this so-called Messiah.

The Greeks "approached Philip and put this request to him: Sir, we would like to see Jesus. Philip went to tell Andrew; Philip and Andrew in turn came to inform Jesus." (John 12:20 ff.).

Why did the Greeks choose Philip and Andrew? Was it by chance? Were they the handiest of the disciples? Or was it because these two apostles had been actively calling people to Jesus? Did they seem eager to have people meet Jesus?

Of all the disciples, including Peter, Philip and Andrew, according to New Testament accounts, were the only two who, once meeting Jesus, immediately ran off to call someone else to him (John 1:35 ff.). Andrew went to fetch Peter; Philip, Nathanael.

I like to think that it was no accident that the Greeks sought out Philip and Andrew. These two were evangelizers, active promoters of Jesus from the moment of their calling.

Perhaps one measure of a committed Christian is the number of people who come up to her or him and ask, "Why are you a believer?" or "Can you explain your faith in Jesus to me?" or "How can you believe in a good God when there is so much evil in the world?"

If we believe in Jesus, we call people to come to meet him.

In our parish, the young adults have a special outreach. It is called the Lamp Post Café. The Lamp Post Café provides young adults, married and single, between the ages of nineteen and thirty-five with an alternative to the bar scene.

Every second Saturday of every month, some twenty young adults from the Young Marrieds and Singles ministry change the parish social hall into a Parisian café. They serve as cooks, waiters and waitresses, dishwashers, hosts and hostesses. There is always live entertainment—dance bands with "side shows" such as magicians and mimes. The entire staff is all-volunteer—from advance planning, shopping for groceries, running errands, setting up, decorating, paying bills, keeping books and doing dishes.

The Lamp Post Café is not a place for preaching. We have asked several so-called Christian bands to stop witnessing during their performances. The Lamp Post Café is designed to reach people who do not yet know the Lord, people who would never come to a Christian rally or a night of preaching, but people who are looking for a good time without the alcohol and sex hassle of the singles bar.

Invariably, however, a Lamp Post Café customer will ask one of the volunteers, "Hey, how often do you work here and how much do you get paid?" The volunteer will usually say something like, "I work here every month—we all do, and it's all volunteer labor."

The customer then usually will ask, "Why do you do that?" And the volunteer will say, "Let me tell you why," draw up a chair and briefly share her or his faith in the Lord and invite the customer to the Wednesday night fellowship.

When the Young Marrieds and Singles started in 1981, there were only eight young adults coming to fellowship regularly. The Lamp Post Café started in 1983. Now there are as many as eighty young adults at fellowship on Wednesdays. The RENEW program also helped bring in new people. In fact, through YMS and the LPC, several Catholics have found their way back into the church after a period of involvement in fundamentalist groups.

The point of all this is simply to contemporize the story of Philip and Andrew. The young adult leaders in our parish have, each in his or her own way, "seen the Lord" and they can tell others about him.

The French writer Paul Claudel, once said, "He who knows the truth and does not shout it from the rooftops is a liar."

I believe Christians need to think about that bold statement. If we are not calling people to Jesus, do we really believe? If we believe in forgiveness, in eternal life, in the power of Jesus to save, how dare we keep it a secret when Jesus himself commands that we "preach the gospel to all nations"?

I realize that many people, perhaps especially people of the Catholic faith, are afraid to "talk religion"—and I'm glad they are! Evangelization is not "talking religion." Evangelization is sharing faith in a living person who has the power to change lives and to overcome evil.

Religion is a set of rules, a set of doctrines, an organization—and these are good, but they are not the core of faith. Faith is in Jesus. From Jesus flow the Church, doctrines and organization, but we must start with Jesus or religion doesn't make sense. Look at the news on TV. How often do newscasters miss the point when reporting on Catholic matters? They start with doctrines. They do not start with Jesus. They start with the papacy and papal teaching. They do not start with Jesus. In fact, they probably do not believe in Jesus—so how can they make sense of things that pertain to the Church which is born of the heart of Jesus?

I am happy Catholics do not want to talk religion, but I am sad that so many do not want to evangelize.

Once, several years ago, during a parish meeting, a very active Catholic man said of evangelization, "I'm afraid of that word." In my usual timid way I shot back, "Well, you'd better get used to it. The pope has been frantically pushing that word for the last twenty years!"

It takes a lot of getting used to.

I understand why so many people are turned off by the phrase and why they are concerned about offending others.

People are turned off by the word "evangelization" because they have been turned off by so-called evangelizers. In September of 1986, Peg and I were watching a popular TV evangelist slaying people in the spirit by having people place blessed handkerchiefs over their heads. It was a circus, not worship.

Many people have been trapped by self-styled saviors who, with Bible in hand, are determined to shove their own personal brand of salvation down everyone's throat. No wonder people are super-sensitive about sharing their own faith. They have been so offended they do not want to chance offending anyone else.

And good Christian people are often afraid to try to share their faith because they "don't know the Bible well enough" or "don't know theology."

Oh, have I got a Bible passage for you!

Just open your Bibles to Luke 10:4 and following. Read that section of the Gospel. Think about those seventy-two disciples—perhaps, for the most part, what we would call "poor country bumpkins." Their own ignorance wasn't enough of a handicap! Jesus challenged them further: "Carry no purse, no haversack, no sandals. Salute no one on the road." He tells them to eat what is put before them—whatever that may be! He says to stay put in whatever home welcomes them—no advance reservations at the local Best Western! He tells them not to play favorites—talk to the boring and the ugly as well as the exciting and the beautiful! And, by the way, I want you to cure the sick and tell everyone the King-dom of God is at hand.

What happened? The seventy-two disciples "returned in jubila-tion, saying, 'Master, even the demons are subject to us in your name!'"

Take heart. This message is recorded for our sake, to give us courage, to show us the secret to sharing our faith effectively.

The first thing that impresses me about this passage from Luke is Jesus telling his disciples not to make all kinds of plans but to go forward with nothing but faith in him. When it comes to sharing God's Word, we need nothing but God's Word, and that Word im-planted deeply and firmly in our hearts. We must know Jesus and love him. We must trust him.

Remember the gifts of the Spirit. Remember the gift of Fortitude that helps us overcome timidity; remember the gift of Counsel that puts the Lord's Word in our minds, in our hearts and on our lips.

Go. Take nothing but the Lord as you know him. If your faith is as small as a mustard seed, it is large enough. Small faith, ignorant people, weak sinners—these are the Lord's favorite tools. Through these tools he works miracles. Remember, too, what St. Paul said: in our weaknesses we are made strong by the very strength of God. Paul boasted of his weakness because it was his weakness, his Middle, his space between the rock and a hard place, through which the Lord poured forth his strength.

If we know nothing but still go forth in faith and the Spirit empowers us, then we and all others will know the strength and the wisdom and the beauty and the love of the Lord. It is better for God, it gives God more glory, for us to be ignorant and humble rather than well informed and proud.

Why be afraid? If we are concerned only with the Lord's glory, we do not fear being foolish for his sake, being, as Paul said, "fools for Christ." It is only when we are concerned with how we look, our own glory, reputation, feelings and popularity that we think about our limitations and ignorance.

I have seen so many "little people" standing tall in faith. Theirs is such a genuine faith. As one dear lady so often says, in her Hispanic accent, "He is so beeeeg!"

If we know Jesus, we will serve him. If we know him and love him and he says, "Cure the sick," we will cure the sick. We will stretch forth our hands and touch the sick, fully expecting Jesus to heal the people through their and our faith.

Jesus has a good track record. We can trust him.

Another lesson from this passage of Luke comes with the full force of a God who wants to be known as God. The disciples were boasting over the way demons fled them when they used Jesus' name. There may have been a little pride creeping into their fledgling ministries.

Jesus, who loved them so very much, put them in their place for their own good: "So," he said to them (paraphrased and interpreted), "you did real well didn't you? You speak my name and the demons flee! Bravo for you! But remember, you disciples, I was with the Father before time began, when Satan, the rebellious angel, fell from heaven! Oh sure, I've given you power over demons and sickness and even poisonous snakes—but all that is of secondary importance. What is important is that you love and obey God so your name can stay in the book of life. Don't get carried away with your ministry. Your ministry is only my tool, my avenue of grace for people. But I am your Way to life. Don't fall in love with your ministry. Love me, the Giver of gifts, the Savior."

Can you imagine what would happen in the world if even 10 percent of Christians woke up tomorrow morning determined to share their faith, in humility and love, with people who do not know Jesus?

Actually, I began this book by sharing my own faith. I have shared my faith throughout, for better or worse, hoping and praying all along that it was God doing the sharing through me and not me sharing my own caricature of God.

Your story is important to others. Your story can bring people closer to Jesus. God needs you so much—you, the priest; you the career woman, the housewife, the teen-age girl, the single mother, the divorcee, the widow; you the lumberjack, the lawyer, the super-jock, the ninety-pound weakling. God needs your story.

Your story is part of his revelation. His Gospel rooted in you is a special word about the Word, a word spoken to the people who share your life—the friends, the bullies, co-workers, bill collectors, doctors, waiters. You, a word about the Word, are spoken from the mouth of God. How humble is our God. He has spoken us— and we have the power to refuse to share his love; we can sin and drive him into hiding, away from our eyes and our lips; we can lie about him, twist our faith-story to make it sound better (as so many of us do, as though we can improve on what God has actually done!). We can ignore him, refuse to believe the word that is us, our faith, the spoken word of God that makes you you and me me.

Of course, when sharing our faith, when speaking in the Lord's name, we must use our heads. We have to realize that we are only filters—and so are those TV evangelists and charismatic fundamentalists who themselves try to pontificate while they deny the role of the pope! We have to realize that the Gospel will be presented by each Christian according to her or his own understanding, faith-experience and, yes, theology.

Everyone has a theology. Even if all you say is, "I believe in God," you have admitted to theology; so don't believe all those people who preach the Gospel and condemn theology. Condemnation of theology is itself a theology. When fundamentalist anti-Catholics condemn the Catholic Church for teaching Tradition, they are speaking from their own tradition.

The Jesuit priest Father Johannes Hofinger has said it very well in his book, *Evangelization and Catechesis*. Father Hofinger says you can't evangelize without teaching your own theology and you can't teach your theology without evangelizing.

When I speak to a congregation about Jesus, I invariably talk about the Church. To me, Jesus and Church are inseparable. I preach the Gospel within the context of a sacramental faith and of a Church with authoritative Tradition. I cannot evangelize without catechizing, without imparting, however indirectly, my theology, my own personal brand of Catholic Gospel-faith.

When I teach people about the Catholic faith, I cannot help but evangelize. How else explain the sacraments but through the saving action of Jesus, or the papacy but through the action of Jesus in speaking to Peter, or the Bible itself without Jesus' presence in his Word and Church?

This is the only caution I give to people who will share their faith or the faith of others. Beware of the filters. Recognize the filters. If you are a Catholic, I will generally trust your filter. If you are a fundamentalist anti-Catholic bigot, I will not trust your filter, your theology, your catechesis.

I know a lady who is like a sponge. She will listen to anyone who says, "Jesus is Lord." She has a beautiful personal trust in Jesus, and this saves her. She is utterly simple. However, I know others who, with more education and sophistication, really get their heads in a mess because they try to soak up everything every preacher says—and the Lord knows how often preachers contradict one another and the Lord as well!

But please! There is so much evil in the world, please speak about Jesus, even if your filter is a little clogged. We need more witnesses out there to counteract those who propagate porn, drugs, child molestation, prostitution, rape, murder and secularism in all of its manifestations.

"Okay," you say, "I do want to evangelize, to share my faith. I am willing to be a fool for Jesus—but can't you give me a little help?"

Perhaps one thing more—besides telling you to read your Bible and develop a good prayer life: know your world as well as your Lord.

1. *In our world are many people who have been seduced by some modern psychologists.* They have been told they can heal themselves, overcome guilt by themselves. They have been told they are their own source of truth, that they can set up their own moral law, that their pleasure and comfort are the most important things in life, that if it feels right or good, do it.

William Kirk Kilpatrick has written a very helpful book, *Psychological Seduction*, that successfully challenges this kind of modern psychology.

When you try to share your faith, you will be dealing with people who have more faith in themselves, government, political parties, economic systems or doctors than they do in God. And you'll find these people in church every Sunday.

Sometimes psychologists treat prayer and God like part of an illness instead of the only solution.

2. *Realize that Christians, and I am speaking here especially of Catholic Christians, are undergoing a crisis in faith—and that makes your job of evangelization all the more difficult.*

Some time ago, I interviewed Archbishop Pio Laghi, the apostolic pro nuncio to the U.S. The interview took place shortly after Cardinal Ratzinger made his famous critique on the Church in several countries. It had been widely reported that Cardinal Ratzinger had severely criticized Catholics in the U.S., saying that we were caught up in secularism.

I asked Archbishop Laghi about that statement and his reaction to it.

He said that the cardinal had addressed the problem of the Church throughout the world. In his evaluation of the Church in the U.S., said Archbishop Laghi, Cardinal Ratzinger said that here Catholics have a crisis of faith in God as Trinity. He said that the humanity of Jesus had been so emphasized that people were forgetting about his divinity and therefore about his relationship with the Father and the Spirit.

The cardinal also saw great danger in people interpreting scripture apart from the Church—and in all fairness, I think we will have to admit that an appreciable number of Catholics have gone over to fundamentalism simply because they did not stay in touch with the Tradition of the Church. They seem to forget that there would be no Bible as we know it today had it not been for the Catholic Church.

Cardinal Ratzinger also cautioned U.S. Catholics against regarding the Church merely as a human institution. He said that Catholics in this country were losing their sense of the Church's mystery. I presume that mass media have had a lot to do with that.

Finally, Archbishop Laghi said that Cardinal Ratzinger was concerned that the great affluence in America is making Christians develop a false sense of security, that in such security, Christians easily forget about God's providence and dominion.

Well, I thought at the time that the cardinal was right on the money and I still do.

When you begin to try to share your faith, you must realize the challenges these factors place before you. In fact, they are within you. We are all affected by a crisis in faith, by the temptation to be our own interpreter of scripture and doctrine, by the humanness of the Church and by affluence.

Realize, too, that you are calling people to conversion to Jesus Christ, not to a theology, a prayer group or a preacher. You are not their God. You are not their savior. Their faith, once they receive it from God, will be expressed through their own filter. They will become evangelizers, preachers, teachers, disciples who seek to cast out demons in the name of Jesus.

Try to understand the faith level of people you hope to bring to Jesus. How much do they already believe? Are they already, in some degree, converted? Are they converted to the basic belief that God exists? Do they realize there is some sort of "holy mystery" out there?

Or is their level of conversion a little deeper? Do they actually believe that Jesus came, that he is Savior? And, if so, have they experienced a conversion to the Church, or to a church? Finding Jesus means finding Church. Following this conversion to Church, people usually enter into a period of moral conversion. They want to behave according to his teachings.

You see, it is not enough to speak only of conversion in a

general sense. Conversion is an ongoing process. Conversion happens when an evangelist introduces someone to Jesus and tells of his saving love. But conversion happens each day as that person falls, repents and rises again, as that person develops her or his own theology, catechesis, philosophy.

I recommend a tremendous book called *A New Look at Preaching*. It contains several talks given at a preaching symposium in Atlanta in 1983. One of the talks is by Father Edward J. Braxton. He speaks clearly on these various levels of conversion. I found his presentation both eloquent and motivating. I have asked myself, time and again, where am I on the coversion scale?

Pope Paul VI, in his 1976 document, "On the Evangelization of Peoples," gave the Christian Church a great teaching on evangelizing. It begs to be read by any Christian interested in bringing more people into a deeper relationship with Jesus.

Paul VI said that evangelization is concerned with the renewal of all humanity. He saw the need for justice in the world. He apparently believed that to preach the Gospel was also to help people escape oppression and poverty in this life.

The pope said that evangelization must occur in all strata of society, in all parts of the world. No one class or nation is without need for hearing the Word of God, of being evangelized.

One of his most important points is that Christians first of all evangelize by the witness of their lives. If they are faithful to the Lord, their lives will call other people to the Lord. A friend of mine once told me about a man in his neighborhood who became a Catholic simply because he saw his Catholic neighbors going to Mass, as a family, on all Sundays and holy days. The witness of life!

Paul VI said, however, that there is great need for "explicit proclamation," the actual sharing of faith in the family and in the marketplace.

He also said that God's Word calls people into community. You cannot believe in God and remain apart from other believers. I was shocked to see on local TV news one evening a story about a preacher who holds services in an abandoned drive-in theater. People stay in their cars to worship "and don't have to feel uncomfortable sitting next to strangers in a church"! For crying out loud!

What kind of Christianity is that? Probably the same kind that motivates some Catholics to avoid giving others the sign of peace during Mass.

The fact that so many Catholics are afraid to offend others when they think about evangelization is a big plus for the Catholic Church. If we can get sensitive people excited about sharing their faith, they will do well.

Father Bob DeShaies, an evangelizing priest here in the U.S., once said that "the unchurched are strangers looking for a friend."

You know, that basically describes what my young adult friends at St. Mary Magdalen's Lamp Post Café are doing. Hardly any of them are well versed in scripture; none have had training as ministers or evangelists. They simply sit down with other young adults and become their friends. They listen to problems with a sympathetic ear. They can identify personally with loneliness, the need for intimacy, the need for meaningful work. They can empathize and be friends. And more. They can, in a helpful, nonthreatening and positive way, share their faith, however small they may think it is.

"The unchurched are strangers looking for a friend."

That is such a beautiful thought.

People, afraid and lonely, caught in their respective Middles, suffering from loneliness, from broken marriages, from cancer, from emotional distress—all looking for a friend.

People, caught in the middle of financial crises, people out of work, people suffering grief and doubting God, people wondering if God is real as they look upon a world torn by crime, war, fear, hate—all people looking for a friend.

And you, in your own Middle, discovering God hanging in there with you, you can be a friend. You can hold a hand. You can offer comfort, encouragement. You can help people find work. You can, in the Middle of this struggle with problems, tell them how you found God in your Middle.

That, my friends, is what evangelization is all about—helping people find God in the Middle, where they are caught in pain and darkness.

The Middle, I have said, is a holy place, a sacred place, a place where we find ourselves, our friends, our strengths, our weaknesses—and our God.

God needs Christians willing to jump in the Middles of the world, to walk the sad walk of the bereaved, the searching walk of the young, the lonely walk of the aged, the painful walk of the sick and dying.

That is what Mother Teresa does. She saw millions of unloved poor people dying. She jumped into the Middle of all that suffering. One little old woman and a handful of her Sisters tackled a mammoth task. But with true humility they were content to embrace only one dying person at a time. They realized they were not God. They could not hold everyone at once in their arms. But they were faithful to the call to do what they could do. They could help one, then two, then ten, then one hundred. And so the ministry grew, became worldwide, because one little woman had the humility and the guts to do a little thing in the face of a great need. She held one dying person—and the world responded.

That is what Mother Angelica does. She saw millions of Catholics losing their faith, going from day to day without learning how to pray, how to grow in faith. She jumped into the Middle of TV evangelization, with no expertise, no money and no plans—only a desire to do what God was asking her to do. She didn't look back. And now, the Church is taking note and responding.

And that is what so many little people do—the deacon who runs a soup kitchen, the group of laywomen who run a pregnancy counseling service for unwed women, the archbishop who promised to pay delivery expenses for women who chose not to have an abortion, the mother of a large family who takes in foster children, the couple who adopts abused children.

Oh, there are so many saints running around we would be hard-pressed to count them. They are people caught in the middle of life, just as we all are, but people who have reached within to touch God and then reached out to touch others.

If we are to serve God, if we are to grow in holiness, we must embrace our Middle, just as Jesus embraced the Cross—for being caught in the middle is indeed the cross of every Christian—the Middle, where we, purified of faith in self, finally embrace our only hope, Jesus Christ, the Lord.

Amen.